Passport to Spanish

CHARLES BERLITZ

Travel Information Supplied
by David Butwin

A SIGNET BOOK

NEW AMERICAN LIBRARY

TIMES MIRROR

Copyright © 1972 by Charles-François Bertin

Library of Congress Catalog Card Number: 79-142436

Published by arrangement with Charles Berlitz.

 SIGNET TRADEMARK REG. U.S. PAT. OFF. AND FOREIGN COUNTRIES
REGISTERED TRADEMARK—MARCA REGISTRADA
HECHO EN CHICAGO, U.S.A.

SIGNET, SIGNET CLASSICS, MENTOR, PLUME, MERIDIAN AND NAL
BOOKS *are published by The New American Library, Inc.,*
1633 Broadway, New York, New York 10019

First Printing, April, 1974

8 9 10 11 12 13 14 15 16

PRINTED IN THE UNITED STATES OF AMERICA

Contents

Travel Information

There is something intoxicating about Spain, something that draws people from afar and won't let them go. How many visitors have uttered the litany, "Spain was so good I had to force myself to leave or I'd still be there." Not to be discounted as one of the allures is the almost unparalleled (at least in Europe) cost of living. As a result, Spain attracts more budget-conscious travelers than does any other country on the Continent. Which brings up the point that a visitor looking for the indelibly Spanish side of Spain will not find it, generally, near the glittering beaches, where the land and customs have been largely preempted by foreigners. Inland, though, traditional Spain still exists. It is hard to imagine a country where unalloyed joy and unmitigated sorrow are so much a part of everyday life, a fact that enriches the traveler's experience and contributes to the mystique that has always been Spain's.

Where to Stay

Nowhere on the Continent will you find better hotel bargains than in Spain. And that applies to Madrid, whose Hotel Ritz, ranked among Europe's top ten and rated grand deluxe by the government, charges only $15 for a single, $20-$26 for a double. All across Spain, $2 or $3 will fetch a room with one and sometimes two stars under the nationally established rating system.

The Spanish government not only regulates all prices but also operates an extensive network of its own hotels, much like the *pousadas* of Portugal. Any branch of the Spanish National Tourist Office will supply maps thickly dotted with locations of such hotels, classified as *paradors, albergues,* or *refugios,* in descending order of style and price. The standard rates, varying only slightly throughout the country, are $8 to $9 for a double and $5 for a single.

Spain operates about eighty-five paradors, which are seldom located at the heart of things. In design, atmosphere, and food, paradors follow the style of the region. Meals are always served, but they are not included in the price. So for $5 you can wake up in a reconstituted palace or castle dating back to medieval days. Among the most striking are the paradors of San Francisco in Granada, of Gibralfaro in Málaga, of Santa Catalina in Jaén, and the Aiguablava parador on the Costa Brava.

Two highly recommended paradors are *Raimundo de Borgoña* in the eleventh-century walled city of Ávila and *Carlos V* in Cáceres. The former, sixty-eight miles west of Madrid, stands above the sun-dried plains of Castile. The city walls were erected in the Middle Ages after the Christians, under King Alfonso VI, regained Ávila from the occupying Muslims. Today the inn, originally the Palacio de Piedras Albas, or the White Stone Palace, has twenty-seven double rooms, all with baths. There are cloisters, wood and stone friezes, and a tower that overlooks a pine-shaded courtyard paved with slabs of granite.

The *Carlos V* is set among the foothills of Extremadura, along the Portuguese border. The converted fifteenth-century stone castle, once inhabited by Charles V, has nineteen double and four single rooms, a series of square and round towers, and an ornamented stone patio where troops once were mustered. An upper story of one wing has three large halls decorated with old arms and rich paintings. You eat in a dining room hung with candlelight chandeliers.

A second kind of accommodation, *albergues*, incorporates many of the paradors' ideas, such as regional decor; but, actually, albergues are closer to motels while paradors correspond to hotels. Rooms come a little cheaper —about $5-$6 for a double, $3.50 for a single, without meals. Also, albergues are distinctly twentieth century and limit guests to a forty-eight-hour stay. One reason is that many albergues are so out of the way there is no other lodging available; so space has to be periodically cleared.

Amenities are substantial, however, usually including restaurant, bar, private baths, hot water. Choice albergues (fifteen altogether) are located in Villacastín, Manzanares (in La Mancha), and Villa Franca del Bierzo.

A third type of government-operated lodging is the *refugio*, often set in mountains or outlands, sometimes near ski areas. Other inexpensive accomodations can be had in the pensions that honeycomb the country and whose prices undercut all others. *Albergues juveniles*, or youth hostels, require youth hostel membership cards, impose a three-night maximum, and require that you register before 8:00 P.M. and bring your own sheets or sleeping bag.

BRUJULA, Spain's official room-finding service, has offices sprinkled throughout the country, especially at train stations and airports. For a small fee they will call ahead and secure reservations. Tourist offices provide information on available space but won't handle the business of booking. Even in the height of summer, rooms are easy to find, although reservations are needed for the popular paradors and albergues.

How to Eat

Eating is another inexpensive Spanish delight. Meals are often included in the price of a hotel room, except in government-run accommodations. The government ranks all restaurants, and all are law-bound to offer a *menú turístico*, or tourist menu, at a controlled price, making it possible to walk into some of the best restaurants in Madrid and order a grand meal at a scaled-down price.

Regional cuisine with ambience prevails not only at paradors and albergues but also at *hosterías*—less common, but worth the search. If a pub captures the English spirit and a bistro describes the French, then a hostería brings you closest to the Spanish. Amid authentic Spanish style, you get a $3 lunch that only a three-hour siesta will cure. One hostería occupies a patch of land at the thirteenth-century university in Alcalá de Henares. By the grand design of Spanish tourism, hosterías are sometimes in remote places entirely new to visitors. A hostería is best for lunch.

Another way to eat your way through Spain is to drift from one *taverna* to the next, pausing long enough for a glass of *Sangría*, or a few Iberian snacks called *tapas*—a potato omelet, *calameres* (squid), kidneys in wine, anchovies, olives. In old Madrid, an ideal tavern-hopping district is near Arco de Cuchilleros. About a dollar brings wine, tapas, and an earful of guitar music.

How to Travel

An encouraging note about Spain's national rail system RENFE: it's been improved. The Talgo and Ter trains run up the best records, and both have air conditioning. Both, too, are express, and thus cost more than the milk runs, but you can ride second class. Since distances between Spain's major cities are so spread out, a bus ride isn't usually worth the money it saves. Flying within Spain—by Aviaco, Iberia's subsidiary, Air Spain, or Spantax—can double the cost of a trip, but depending on the distance and the terrain, a plane is a wise choice. It cuts time and monotony but may rob the traveler of the local color he is certain to encounter on a train. On all trains except the Talgo and Ter, passengers must switch at the border because of a difference in track size. Hitchhiking, while not forbidden, isn't done—rides are hard to wangle.

What to Buy

In Spain the best shopping bargains are in the larger cities. Spanish *artesanía* (handicrafts) may seem irresistible in a south coast fishing village, but department stores in Madrid and Barcelona will consistently offer better meals. Lately the national tourist office has unofficially and temporarily blacklisted certain major stores because of their

failure to ship products overseas; so you are advised to
check first. Madrid's Los Guerrilleros on the Punta del Sol
may be the world's largest shoe store, and it's full of $2
and $3 pairs. Tumult and shouting prevail at Madrid's
Rastro, or flea market, which is open daily but at its peak
on Sunday. Barcelona's market unfolds in the Gothic
Quarter, while Seville has a smaller, less spectacular dis-
play.

Among the bargains to hunt for in Spain are hand-
tooled guitars for $10 or less, carved olivewood objects
such as boxes and letter openers, and wrought-iron trivets.
In Granada: filigree gold and silver, rugs with distinctive
white backgrounds and colorful patterns (dragons and geo-
metric designs appear often) of the Moorish influence. In
Seville: multicolored tiles, *azulejos*. Toledo: embroidery
and Toledo steel (turned into bullfighter's swords, manicure scissors, razor blades). And anywhere: suede and
leather goods for half the U.S. cost.

What to Do

In Madrid, a ramble might begin in the morning with a
visit to the Prado, where about 50 cents opens the doors
to 3,000 of the world's greatest paintings, including Goya's
The Naked Maja, Velázquez's *Las Meninas*, and a number
of El Grecos. Afternoon bullfights are in season from early
spring through October. The least expensive seats for any
corrida are classified *sol* (sun), medium-priced *sol-y-
sombra* (sun and shade), and most expensive *sombra*
(shade). Ticket prices vary with the skill of the fighter.
Sol seats for a rookie or lackluster performer might be
under $1, while *sombra* seats will draw $8 when El Cor-
dobès fights. Beware: scalpers are merciless.

Spanish frenzy also boils over at jai-alai or *pelota* con-
tests, nightly except Monday at 10:45 at Fronton Madrid.
Seats go for under 50 cents. Bets are exchanged feverishly,
recalling the atmosphere of Hialeah in the first race. In
Basque towns, *pelota* is performed in the main squares.

Many of Spain's wonders lie within easy distance of Madrid. Toledo, three hours by train from Madrid, is quiet and serene, reflecting few of the somber visions of El Greco, adopted son. The Santo Tomé Church, the House and Museum of El Greco, and the Museo de Santa Cruz all contain his paintings. Admission to the cathedral, open daily, is less than a quarter. Seville, the setting of such operas as *Don Giovanni, Carmen,* and *The Barber of Seville,* has always touched the heart. No less now than in centuries past, Seville brims with flowing mantillas, orange trees, parks, and gardens. The city's pièce de résistance is the Giralda Tower, built by twelfth-century Moors as a minaret; it affords a splendid 10-cent view of the city.

Spain's fabled free attractions are its ocean beaches. Beautiful People, hippies, and Spaniards stream into Palma on the Balearic Island of Mallorca and into Marbella and Torremolinos on the Costa del Sol. The beaches are less crowded on the lesser-known Balearics, such as Formentera, and on the Costa de la Luz, which runs along the Atlantic from the Straits of Gibraltar to the Portuguese border.

Barcelona is a ten-hour train ride from Madrid and often too far away for most tourists—perhaps a blessing. In other words, things are cheaper and easier to get into. Barcelona's Ensanche, or newer part, has neatly planted trees and fountains, while the Gothic Quarter is crowded with medieval stone houses and narrow, shop-lined streets. The Picasso Museum, already a showcase of his work, has recently been enriched by a donation of new Picassos.

DAVID BUTWIN

NOTE: *Prices in dollars will vary according to whatever rate of exchange is in effect at a given time.*

🔲 Preface

Is it possible to learn to speak Spanish from a phrase book? If one means basic communication—the ability to speak, understand, and generally get along—the answer is "yes," *if* you learn the right phrases. The secret of learning languages is to learn not only individual words, but the phrases in which they are apt to occur on a frequency basis, as the Spanish use them every day.

The purpose of this book is to provide instant communication in Spanish. The phrases are short, geared to situations of daily life, and pinpointed for easy reference, so that you can find the exact section you need at any moment.

There is even a chapter—"Words That Show You Are 'With It'"—which gives you the key words and phrases that Spanish people use to add color to their conversation. In this way, instead of learning about "the umbrella of my aunt," you learn to use the right phrase at the right time, in the very way a Spanish person would use it. And, so that Spanish people will understand your accent, all you have to do is read the phonetic line under each Spanish phrase *as if it were English*. Further practice and listening to Spanish people speaking will constantly improve your accent.

The use of this book is not limited to a trip to Spain or Latin America or other parts of the Spanish-speaking world. Spanish is spoken throughout the world, and, besides the pleasure and help you will get by speaking Spanish on your travels, you will find it an additional pleasure to use the idiomatic Spanish you will learn in this book in Spanish restaurants and with Spanish-speaking people you may meet anywhere.

Young people studying Spanish in a more conventional manner in school or college will find this book an invaluable aid to their studies in that it brings modern colloquial Spanish alive as a means of communication.

The use of this book will more than double your enjoyment of a trip abroad and also help you save money. Besides the economic factor, why visit a foreign country if you can't break the language barrier and communicate with the new and interesting people you meet? You might as well stay home and see the palaces and monuments of the country on color TV. Who wants to be limited to one language when picking up another language can be so easy and enjoyable?

One can speak and understand current everyday Spanish with comparatively few words and phrases—perhaps 1500 to 1800—which is less than the number given in the special dictionary at the end of this book. By using the same short constructions over and over, in the various situations where they normally occur, you will acquire them without conscious effort. They will become a part of your own vocabulary and of your memory bank, and that is, after all, the only secret of learning a language.

How to Acquire an Instant Spanish Accent

Every word or sentence in this book is presented in English, in Spanish, and in an easy-to-read pronunciation system to help you say the Spanish correctly. Just pronounce the third line as if you were reading English. Stress the syllables printed in capital letters.

English: **Do you speak Spanish?**
Spanish: **¿Habla Usted español?**
Pronunciation: *¿AH-bla oo-STED ess-pahn-YOHL?*

Although the following points are made clear in the third line, they will be helpful for you in pronouncing and reading Spanish generally:

The vowels a, e, i, o, u are pronounced *ah, eh, ee, oh, oo* respectively. In our pronunciation system, we have added an *h* to some syllables, such as *do* and *to*, to remind you to pronounce them *doh* and *toh* and not to confuse them with the sounds of the English words "do" and "to." (Note that *i* standing alone in the pronunciation line represents the sound of the English word "I" or "eye.")

Ll is pronounced like the *lli* in *million*.

ñ in pronounced like the *ny* in *canyon*.

j is pronounced like the English *h*.

g before *e* and *i* is also pronounced like the English *h* but with a stronger and more gutteral sound.

The Spanish h is silent.

The combination *ay* or *ai* is pronounced like the English word "I."

In most parts of Spain c before e or i, or z before any letter, is pronounced like the English *th* in *think*, rather like a lisp. In southern Spain and in Latin America these letters generally sound like an *s*. We have written them as *s* in the pronunciation line because this is easier to say and more widely used.

And, finally, to approximate an authentic Spanish or

Latin American way of speaking, be sure to roll the r, especially the double rr.

With this advice, and the easy pronunciation reminder under each word, you are almost certain to be told: ¡*Usted tiene un acento muy bueno!* ¡oo-STED T'YEH-neh oon ah-SEN-toh mwee BWEH-no! Which means: "You have a very good accent!"

1. Greetings and Introductions

When addressing people call them **Señor, Señora, or Señorita** with or *without* adding their last names. Even when you say simply **Buenos días** ("Good morning" or "Good day") it is more polite to add one of these titles to it.

Mr. (or) Sir
Señor
sen-YOR

Mrs. (or) Madam
Señora
sen-YO-ra

Miss
Señorita
sen-yo-REE-ta

Good morning, sir.
Buenos días, señor.
BWEH-nohs DEE-yahs, sen-YOR.

Good afternoon, madam.
Buenas tardes, señora.
BWEH-nahs TAR-dehs sen-YO-ra.

Good evening, miss.
Buenas noches, señorita.
BWEH-nahs NO-chehs, sen-yo-REE-ta.

How are you?
¿Cómo está usted?
¿KO-mo ess-TA oo-STED?

Very well, thank you. And you?
Muy bien, gracias. ¿Y usted?
mwee b'yen, GRA-s'yahs. ¿ee oo-STED?

Come in.
Adelante.
ah-deh-LAHN-teh.

Sit down, please.
Siéntese, por favor.
S'YEN-teh-seh, por fa-VOR.

I am Robert Gómez.
Yo soy Roberto Gómez.
yo soy ro-BEHR-toh GO-mess.

Your name, please?
¿Su nombre, por favor?
¿soo NOHM-breh, por fa-VOR?

May I introduce . . .	Very happy to meet you.
Le presento a . . .	Mucho gusto.
leh preh-SEN-toh ah . . .	*MOO-cho GOO-sto.*
Good-bye.	So long.
Adiós.	·Hasta luego.
ah-D'YOHS.	*AH-sta LWEH-go.*

A propósito (By the way): The word for "you"—usted— is almost always written in the abbreviated form **Ud.** or **Vd.** In future sections we will write it this way since this is how you will see it.

2. Basic Expressions

Learn the following expressions by heart. You will use them every time you speak Spanish to someone. If you memorize these expressions and the numbers in the next section you will find that you can ask prices, directions, and generally make your wishes known.

Yes.	No.	Perhaps.	Of course.
Sí.	No.	Quizá.	Por supuesto.
see.	*no.*	*kee-SA.*	*por soo-PWESS-toh.*

Please.	Thank you.	You are welcome.
Por favor.	Gracias.	De nada.
por fa-VOR.	*GRA-s'yahs.*	*deh NA-da.*

Pardon.	I'm sorry.	It's all right.
Perdón.	Lo siento.	Está bien.
pehr-DOHN.	*lo S'YEN-toh.*	*ess-TA b'yen.*

Here.	There.	This.	That.
Aquí.	Allí.	Esto.	Eso.
ah-KEE.	*ahl-YEE.*	*ESS-toh.*	*ES-so.*

Do you speak English?	I speak Spanish a little.
¿Habla Ud. inglés?	Hablo español un poco.
¿AH-bla oo-STED een-GLEHS?	*AH-blo ess-pahn-YOHL oon PO-ko.*

Do you understand?	I understand.
¿Comprende Ud.?	Yo comprendo.
¿kom-PREN-deh oo-STED?	*yo kom-PREN-doh.*

I don't understand.	Very well.
Yo no comprendo.	Muy bien.
yo no kom-PREN-doh.	*mwee b'yen.*

When?
¿Cuándo?.
¿KWAHN-doh?

How far?
¿A qué distancia?
¿ah keh dees-TANH-s'ya?

How much time?
¿Cuánto tiempo?
¿KWAHN-toh T'YEM-po?

How?
¿Cómo?
¿KO-mo?

Why not?
¿Cómo no?
¿KO-mo no?

Like this.
Así.
ah-SEE.

Not like that.
Así no.
ah-SEE no.

It is possible.
Es posible.
ess po-SEE-bleh.

It is not possible.
No es posible.
no ess po-SEE-bleh.

Now.
Ahora.
ah-OH-ra.

Not now.
Ahora no.
ah-OH-ra no.

Later.
Más tarde.
mahs TAR-deh.

That's fine.
Está bien.
ess-TA b'yen.

It's very good.
Es muy bueno.
ess mwee BWEH-no.

It's not good.
No es bueno.
no ess BWEH-no.

It doesn't matter.
No importa.
no eem-POR-ta.

It's very important.
Es muy importante.
ess mwee eem-por-TAHN-teh.

Speak slowly, please.
Hable despacio, por favor.
AH-bleh deh-SPA-s'yo, por fa-VOR.

Repeat, please.
Repita, por favor.
reh-PEE-ta, por fa-VOR.

Write it, please.
Escríbalo, por favor.
Es-KREE-ba-lo, por fa-VOR.

Who is it?	Come in.	Don't come in!
¿Quién es?	Entre:	¡No entre!
¿k'yen ess?	EN-treh.	¡no EN-treh!

Stop.	Wait.	Let's go.	That's all.
Pare.	Espere.	Vamos.	Eso es todo.
PA-reh.	ess-PEH-reh.	VA-mohs.	ES-so ess TOH-doh.

What is this?	Where is the telephone?
¿Qué es esto?	¿Dónde está el teléfono?
¿keh ess ESS-toh?	¿DOHN-deh ess-TA el teh-LEH-fo-no?

Where is the (rest) room?
¿Dónde está el cuarto?
¿DOHN-deh ess-TA el KWAHR-toh?

... for ladies?	... for men?
... para damas?	... para caballeros?
... PA-ra DA-mahs?	... PA-ra ka-bahl-YEH-rohs?

Show me.	How much?	It's too much.
Muéstreme.	¿Cuánto?	Es demasiado.
MWEHS-treh-meh.	¿KWAHN-toh?	ess deh-ma-S'YA-doh.

Who?	I	you	he	she
¿Quién?	yo	usted	él	ella
¿k'yen?	yo	(Ud.) oo-STED	el	EL-ya

we (men)	we (women)	you (plural)
nosotros	nosotras	ustedes (Uds.)
no-SO-trohs	no-SO-trahs	oo-STED-ehs

they (men)	they (women)
ellos	ellas
EL-yohs	EL-yahs

A propósito: The phrase **por favor,** which you should always use when you ask questions or make requests, can also function for "Bring me . . . ," "I want . . . ," or "I would like . . . ," etc. Simply say **Por favor** followed by the word for whatever you want, which you can find in the dictionary section.

You have noticed that there are separate words for "we" and "they" according to whether you are referring to men or women. If you are referring to a mixed group of men and women, use the masculine.

¿**No?** as a question can be used to request agreement to something or to mean "Isn't it?" "Isn't this right?" "Don't you think so?"

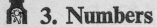 # 3. Numbers

The numbers are important not only for asking prices (and perhaps to bargain) but for phone numbers, addresses, and telling time. Learn the first twenty by heart and then from 20 to 100 by tens, and you can deal with **el dinero** (money), **números de teléfono** (telephone numbers), and **direcciones** (addresses).

1	2	3	4
uno	dos	tres	cuatro
OO-no	*dohs*	*trehs*	*KWA-tro*

5	6	7	8
cinco	seis	siete	ocho
SEEN-ko	*sayss*	*S'YEH-tch*	*OH-cho*

9	10	11	12
nueve	diez	once	doce
N'WEH-veh	*d'yess*	*OHN-seh*	*DOH-seh*

13	14	15	16
trece	catorce	quince	diez y seis
TREH-seh	*ka-TOHR-seh*	*KEEN-seh*	*d'yess ee SAYSS*

17	18	19
diez y siete	diez y ocho	diez y nueve
d'yess ee S'YEH-teh	*d'yess ee OH-cho*	*d'yess ee N'WEH-veh*

20	21	22
veinte	veintiuno	veintidós
VAIN-teh	*vain-tee-OO-no*	*vain-tee-DOHS*

30	31	32
treinta	treinta y uno	treinta y dos
TRAIN-ta	*TRAIN-ta ee OO-no*	*TRAIN-ta ee dohs*

40	**50**	**60**
cuarenta	cincuenta	sesenta
kwa-REN-ta	*seen-KWEN-ta*	*seh-SEN-ta*

70	**80**	**90**
setenta	ochenta	noventa
seh-TEN-ta	*oh-CHEN-ta*	*no-VEN-ta*

100	**200**	**300**
ciento	doscientos	trescientos
S'YEN-toh	*dohs-S'YEN-tohs*	*trehs-S'YEN-tohs*

400	**500**	**600**
cuatrocientos	quinientos	seiscientos
KWA-tro-S'YEN-tohs	*keen-YEN-tohs*	*sayss-S'YEN-tohs*

700	**800**	**900**
setecientos	ochocientos	novecientos
seh-teh-S'YEN-tohs	*OH-choh-S'YEN-tohs*	*no-veh-S'YEN-tohs*

1000	**1,000,000**
mil	un millón
meel	*oon meel-YON*

1st	**2nd**	**3rd**
primero	segundo	tercero
pree-MEH-ro	*seh-GOON-doh*	*tehr-SEH-ro*

the last	**half**	**zero**
el último	medio	cero
el OOL-tee-mo	*MEH-d'yo*	*SEH-ro*

How much?	**How many?**	**What number?**
¿Cuánto?	¿Cuántos?	¿Qué número?
¿KWAHN-toh?	*¿KWAHN-tohs?*	*¿keh NOO-meh-ro?*

4. Arrival

Besides talking with airport officials, one of the most important things you will want to do on arrival in a Spanish-speaking country is to find your way about. For this reason we offer you here some basic "asking your way" questions and answers and call your attention to the "Point to the Answer" sections, which the people to whom you speak can use to *point out* answers to make it easier for you to understand.

Your passport, please.
Su pasaporte, por favor.
soo pa-sa-POR-teh, por fa-VOR.

I am on a visit.
Estoy de visita.
ess-TOY deh vee-SEE-ta.

For three weeks.
Por tres semanas.
por trehs seh-MA-nahs.

I am on a business trip.
Estoy en un viaje de negocios.
ess-TOY en oon V'YA-heh deh neh-GO-s'yohs.

Where is the customs?
¿Dónde está la aduana?
¿DOHN-deh ess-TA la ah-DWA-na?

Where is your baggage?
¿Dónde está su equipaje?
¿DOHN-deh ess-TA soo eh-kee-PA-heh?

My bags are over there.
Mis maletas están allí.
mees ma-LEH-tahs ess-TAN ahl-YEE.

Those over there.
Aquéllas.
ah-KEL-yahs.

This one is mine.
Ésta es mía.
ESS-ta es MEE-ya.

That one.
Esa.
ESS-ah.

Those bags there.
Aquellas maletas.
ah-KEL-yahs ma-LEH-tahs.

Shall I open it?
¿La abro?
¿la AH-bro?

Open it.
Ábrala.
AH-bra-la.

There you are.
Ya.
ya.

One moment, please.
Un momento, por favor.
oon mo-MEN-toh, por fa-VOR.

I am looking for the key.
Estoy buscando la llave.
ess-TOY boos-KAHN-doh la L'YA-veh.

I have nothing to declare.
No tengo nada que declarar.
no TEN-go NA-da keh deh-kla-RAR.

This is for my personal use.
Esto es para mi uso personal.
ESS-toh ess PA-ra me OO-so pehr-so-NAHL.

This has been used.
Esto ha sido usado.
ESS-toh ah SEE-doh oo-SA-doh.

These are gifts.
Éstos son regalos.
ESS-tohs sohn reh-GA-lohs.

Must I pay duty?
¿Debo pagar algo?
¿deh-bo pa-GAR AHL-go?

Where is a telephone?
¿Dónde hay un teléfono?
¿DOHN-deh I oon teh-LEH-fo-no?

Where is the bus to the city?
¿Dónde está el autobús para la ciudad?
¿DOHN-deh ess-TA el ow-toh-BOOS PA-ra la s'yoo-DAHD?

Where is the rest room?
¿Dónde está el lavabo?
*¿DOHN-deh ess-TA el
la-VA-bo?*

Where is a restaurant?
¿Dónde hay un restaurante?
*¿DOHN-deh I oon rest-ow-
RAHN-teh?*

Porter!
¡Maletero!
¡ma-leh-TEH-ro!

Take these bags to a taxi.
Lleve estas maletas a un
taxi.
*L'YEH-veh ESS-tahs
ma-LEH-tahs ah oon
TAHX-see.*

I'll carry this one myself.
Yo me llevo ésta.
yo meh L'YEH-vo ESS-ta.

How much is it?
¿Cuánto es?
¿KWAHN-toh ess?

To the Hotel Liberty.
Al hotel Libertad.
ahl o-TEL lee-ber-TAHD.

To the Hotel Bolívar, please.
Al hotel Bolívar, por favor.
ahl o-TEL bo-LEE-var, por fa-VOR.

How can I go . . .
¿Cómo puedo ir . . .
¿KO-mo PWEH-doh eer . . .

. . . to the Hotel Bolívar?
. . . al hotel Bolívar?
*. . . ahl o-TEL
bo-LEE-var?*

. . . to a good restaurant?
. . . a un buen restaurante?
. . . ah oon bwehn rest-ow-RAHN-teh?

. . . to the American consulate?
. . . al consulado americano?
. . . ahl kohn-soo-LA-doh a-meh-ree-KA-no?

British	Canadian	Australian
británico	canadiense	australiano
bree-TA-nee-ko	*ka-na-D'YEN-seh*	*owss-trahl-YA-no*

... to this address?
... a esta dirección?
... *ah ESS-ta dee-rek-S'YOHN?*

... to the movies?
... al cine?
... *ahl SEE-neh?*

... to the post office?
... al correo?
... *ahl ko-REH-oh?*

... to the police station?
... al cuartel de policía?
... *ahl kwar-TEHL deh po-lee-SEE-ya?*

... to a pharmacy?
... a una farmacia?
... *ah OO-na far-MA-s'ya?*

... to a hospital?
... al hospital?
... *al ohs-pee-TAHL?*

... to a barber?
... al barbero?
... *ahl bar-BEH-ro?*

... to a hairdresser?
... a un salón de belleza?
... *ah oon sa-LOHN deh behl-YEH-sa?*

Follow this street until you get to Independence Street.
Siga esta calle hasta llegar a la calle Independencia.
SEE-ga ESS-ta KAHL-yeh AHS-ta l'yeh-GAR ah la KAHL-yeh een-deh-pen-DEN-s'ya.

To the right.
A la derecha.
ah la deh-REH-cha.

To the left.
A la izquierda.
ah la ees-K'YEHR-da.

On the corner.
En la esquina.
en la ess-KEE-na.

Turn left when you get to the Fifth of May Avenue.
Doble a la izquierda al llegar a la avenida Cinco de Mayo.
DOH-bleh ah la ees-K'YEHR-da ahl yeh-GAR ah la ah-veh-NEE-da SEEN-ko deh MA-yo.

Follow Bolivar Avenue.
Siga por la avenida Bolívar.
SEE-ga por la ah-veh-NEE-da bo-LEE-var.

Is it far?	Yes.	No.	It's near.
¿Es lejos?	Sí.	·No.	Está cerca.·
¿ess LEH-hohs?	*see.*	*no.*	*ess-TA SEHR-ka.*

Thank you very much.
Muchas gracias.
MOO-chahs GRA-s'yahs.

You are very kind.
Es usted muy amable.
ess oo-STED mwee ah-MA-bleh.

A propósito: When you speak to a stranger don't forget to say **Perdón, señor** (or **señora**) before you ask a question. If you speak to a policeman, you can call him **señor** too.

Streets in most Spanish-speaking countries have white-on-blue signs on the buildings at each corner, making it easy to find out where you are.

To make sure you understand people's answers you can show them the "Point to the Answer" section in the back of the book, as well as the shorter·sections in Chapters 5, 8, 10, 11, 12, and 16.

5. Hotel—Laundry— Dry Cleaning

Although the staffs of the larger hotels have some training in English, you will find that the use of Spanish makes for better understanding and better relations, especially with the service personnel. Besides, it is fun, and you should practice Spanish at every opportunity. We have included laundry and dry cleaning in this section as these are things about which you have to make yourself understood in speaking to the hotel chambermaid or valet.

Can you recommend a good hotel?
¿Puede recomendar un buen hotel?
¿PWEH-deh reh-ko-men-DAR oon bwehn oh-TEL?

. . . a guest house?
. . . una casa de huéspedes?
. . . OO-na KA-sa deh WEHS-peh-dess?

In the center of town.
En el centro de la ciudad.
en el SEN-tro de la s'yoo-DAHD.

Not too expensive.
No muy caro.
no mwee KA-ro.

I have a reservation.
Tengo una reservación.
TEN-go OO-na reh-sehr-va-S'YOHN.

My name is _____.
Mi nombre es _____
mee NOHM-breh ess _____.

Have you a room?
¿Tiene una habitación?
¿T'YEH-neh OO-na ah-bee-ta-S'YOHN?

I would like a room . . .
Me gustaría una habitación . . .
meh goo-sta-REE-ya OO-na ah-bee-ta-S'YOHN . . .

. . . for one person.
. . . para una persona.
. . . PA-ra OO-na pehr-SO-na.

. . . for two people.
. . . para dos personas.
. . . PA-ra dohs pehr-SO-nahs.

. . . with two beds.
. . . con dos camas.
. . . kohn dohs KA-mahs.

. . . with a bathroom.
. . . con baño.
. . . kohn BAHN-yo.

. . . with hot water.
. . . con agua caliente.
. . . kohn AH-gwa kahl-YEN-teh.

. . . air conditioned.
. . . aire acondicionado.
. . . I-reh ah-kohn-dee-s'yo-NA-doh.

. . . with a balcony.
. . . con un balcón.
. . . kohn oon bahl-KOHN.

. . . with television.
. . . con televisión.
. . . kohn teh-leh-vee-S'YOHN.

... with a radio.
... con radio.
... *kohn RA-d'yo.*

Two connecting rooms.
Dos habitaciones contiguas.
dohs ah-bee-ta-S'YO-nehs kohn-TEE-gwahs.

How much is it?	... per day?	... per week?
¿Cuánto es?	... por día?	... por semana?
¿*KWAHN-toh ess?*	... *por DEE-ya?*	... *por seh-MA-na?*

Are the meals included?
¿Están incluídas las comidas?
¿ess-TAHN een-kloo-EE-dahs lahs ko-MEE-dahs?

Is breakfast included?
¿Está incluído el desayuno?
¿ess-TA een-kloo-EE-doh el des-ah-YOO-no?

I should like to see it.
Me gustaría verla.
meh goo-sta-REE-ya VEHR-la.

Where is the bath?	... the shower?
¿Dónde está el baño?	... la ducha?
¿*DOHN-deh ess-TA el BAHN-yo?*	... *la DOO-cha?*

I want another room.	... higher up.
Quiero otra habitación.	... más arriba.
K'YEH-ro OH-tra ah-bee-ta-S'YOHN.	... *mahs ah-REE-ba.*

... better.	... larger.	... smaller.
... mejor.	... más grande.	... más pequeña.
... *meh-HOR.*	... *mahs GRAHN-deh.*	... *mahs peh-KEN-ya*

I'll take this room.
Tomo esta habitación.
TOH-mo ESS-ta ah-bee-ta-S'YOHN.

I'll stay for _____ days.
Me quedaré por _____ días.
meh keh-da-REH por _____ DEE-yahs.

What time is lunch served?
¿A qué hora se sirve el almuerzo?
¿ah keh OH-ra seh SEER-veh el ahl-MWEHR-so?

What time is dinner served?
¿A qué hora se sirve la cena?
¿ah keh OH-ra seh SEER-veh la SEH-na?

I would like a bottle of mineral water and ice.
Quisiera una botella de agua mineral y hielo.
kee-S'YEH-ra OO-na bo-TEL-ya deh AH-gwa mee-neh-
    RAHL ee YEH-lo.

Will you send breakfast . . .
Quiere mandar el desayuno . . .
K'YEH-reh mahn-DAR el des-ah-YOO-no . . .

. . . to room number _____.
. . . a la habitación número _____.
. . . ah la ah-bee-ta-S'YOHN NOO-meh-ro _____.

**Orange juice, coffee with
    (hot) milk,**
Jugo de naranja, café con
    leche,
*HOO-go deh na-RAHN-ha,
    ka-FEH kohn LEH-cheh,*

rolls and butter.
panecillas y mantequilla.
*pa-neh-SEEL-yahs ee mahn-
    teh-KEEL-ya.*

(For a more complete breakfast, see page 38.)

Will you send these letters?
¿Quiere mandar estas cartas?
¿K'YEH-reh mahn-DAR ESS-tahs KAR-tahs?

Will you put stamps on them?
¿Quiere ponerles estampillas?
¿K'YEH-reh po-NEHR-lehs ess-tahm-PEEL-yahs?

The key, please.
La llave, por favor.
lah L'YA-veh, por fa-VOR.

Is there any mail for me?
¿Hay correo para mi?
¿I ko-RREH-oh PA-ra mee?

Send my mail to this address.
Mande mi correo a esta dirección.
MAHN-deh mee ko-RREH-oh ah ESS-ta dee-rek-S'YOHN.

I want to speak to the manager.
Quiero hablar con el gerente.
K'YEH-ro ah-BLAR kohn el heh-REN-teh.

I need an interpreter.
Necesito un intérprete.
neh-seh-SEE-toh oon een-TEHR-preh-teh.

Are you the chambermaid?
¿Es usted la camarera?
¿ess oo-STED la ka-ma-REH-ra?

Will you change the sheets?
¿Quiere cambiar las sábanas?
¿K'YEH-reh kahm-B'YAR lahs SA-ba-nahs?

I need a blanket.
Necesito una frazada.
*neh-seh-SEE-toh OO-na
fra-SA-da.*

. . . a pillow.
. . . una almohada.
. . . OO-na ahl-mo-AH-da.

. . . a towel.
. . . una toalla.
*. . . OO-na toh-
AHL-ya.*

. . . soap.
. . . jabón.
. . . ha-BOHN.

. . . toilet paper.
. . . papel
higiénico.
*. . . pa-PEL ee-
H'YEH-nee-ko.*

This is to be cleaned.
Esto es para limpiar.
*ESS-toh ess PA-ra leem-
P'YAR.*

This is to be pressed.
Esto es para planchar.
*ESS-toh ess PA-ra plahn-
CHAR.*

This is to be washed.
Esto es para lavar.
ESS-toh ess PA-ra la-VAR.

This is to be repaired.
Esto es para reparar.
*ESS-toh ess PA-ra
reh-pa-RAR.*

For this evening?
¿Para esta noche?
¿PA-ra ESS-ta NO-cheh?

. . . tomorrow?
. . . mañana?
. . . mahn-YA-na?

. . . tomorrow afternoon?
. . . mañana por la tarde?
*. . . mahn-YA-na por la
TAR-deh?*

. . . tomorrow evening?
. . . mañana por la noche?
*. . . mahn-YA-na por la
NO-cheh?*

When?
¿Cuándo?
¿KWAHN-doh?

For sure?
¿Seguro?
¿seh-GOO-ro?

Be careful with this.
Tenga cuidado con esto.
TEN-ga kwee-DA-doh kohn ESS-toh.

Don't press this with a hot iron.
No planche esto con plancha caliente.
no PLAHN-cheh ESS-toh kohn PLAHN-cha
ka-L'YEN-teh.

The dry cleaner.
La tintorería.
la teen-toh-reh-REE-ya.

Are my clothes ready?
¿Está lista mi ropa?
¿ess-TA LEES-ta mee RRO-pa?

Prepare my bill, please.
Prepare mi cuenta, por favor.
preh-PA-reh mee KWEN-ta, por fa-VOR.

I'm leaving tomorrow morning.
Salgo mañana por la mañana.
SAHL-go mahn-YA-na por la mahn-YA-na.

Will you call me at 7 o'clock?
¿Quiere llamarme a las siete?
¿K'YEH-reh l'ya-MAR-meh ah lahs S'YEH-teh?

It's very important.
Es muy importante.
ess mwee eem-por-TAHN-teh.

A propósito: Hotel floors are generally counted starting
above the ground floor (**piso bajo**), so that the second floor
is called the first, the third the second, etc.

Point to the Answer

Sírvase indicar en esta página su contestación a mi pregunta. Muchas gracias.
Please point on this page to your answer to my question. Thank you very much.

Hoy.	**Esta tarde.**	**Esta noche.**
Today.	This afternoon.	This evening.

Mañana.	**Temprano.**	**Tarde.**
Tomorrow.	Early.	Late.

Antes de la una.	**Antes de las dos,**	tres,	quatro, cinco.
Before one o'clock.	Before two,	three,	four, five o'clock.

A las seis, siete, ocho, nueve, diez, once, doce.
At six, seven, eight, nine, ten, eleven, twelve o'clock.

lunes	**martes**	**miércoles**	**jueves**
Monday	Tuesday	Wednesday	Thursday

viernes	**sábado**	**domingo**
Friday	Saturday	Sunday

6. Time: Hours—Days—
Months

In the "Hotel" section you noted that when making an appointment at a certain hour you simply put a las in front of the number, except for "one o'clock" when you use a la. The following section shows you how to tell time in greater detail, including dates. You can make all sorts of arrangements with people by indicating the hour, the day, or the date, and adding the phrase ¿Está bien?—Is that all right?

What time is it?
¿Qué hora es?
¿keh OH-ra ess?

It is one o'clock.
Es la una.
ess la OO-na.

It is six o'clock.
Son las seis.
sohn lahs sayss.

Half past six.
Las seis y media.
lahs sayss ee MEHD-ya.

A quarter past seven.
Las siete y cuarto.
*lahs S'YEH-teh ee
  KWAHR-toh.*

A quarter to eight.
Ocho menos cuarto.
*OH-cho MEH-nohs
  KWAHR-toh.*

Ten minutes past two.
Dos y diez.
dohs ee d'yess.

Ten minutes to three.
Tres menos diez.
trehs MEH-nohs d'yess.

At nine o'clock.
A las nueve.
ah lahs NWEH-veh.

At exactly nine o'clock.
A las nueve en punto.
*ah lahs NWEH-veh en
  POON-toh.*

the morning
la mañana
la mahn-YA-na

the afternoon
la tarde
la TAR-deh

noon
mediodía
meh-d'yo-DEE-ya

the night	**today**	**tomorrow**
la noche	hoy	mañana
la NO-cheh	*oy*	*mahn-YA-na*

yesterday	**the day after tomorrow**
ayer	pasado mañana
ah-YEHR	*pa-SA-doh mahn-YA-na*

the day before yesterday
anteayer
ahn-teh-ah-YEHR

this evening	**tomorrow evening**
esta noche	mañana por la noche
ESS-ta NO-cheh	*mahn-YA-na por la NO-cheh*

last night	**this week**
ayer por la noche	esta semana
ah-YEHR por la NO-cheh	*ESS-ta seh-MA-na*

last week	**next week**
la semana pasada	la semana próxima
la seh-MA-na pa-SA-da	*la seh-MA-na PROHX-see-ma.*

two weeks ago	**this month**
hace dos semanas	este mes
AH-seh dohs seh-MA-nas	*ESS-teh mess*

several months ago	**this year**
hace algunos meses	este año
AH-seh ahl-GOO-nohs	*ESS-teh AHN-yo*
MEH-sehs	

last year	**next year**
el año pasado	el año próximo
el AHN-yo pa-SA-doh	*el AHN-yo PROHX-see-mo*

five years ago	**1971**	
hace cinco años	mil novecientos setenta y	
AH-seh SEEN-ko AHN-yos	uno	
	meel no-veh-S'YEN-tohs	
	seh-TEN-ta ee oo-no	

Monday	**Tuesday**	**Wednesday**
lunes	martes	miércoles
LOO-nehs	*MAR-tehs*	*M'YER-ko-lehs*

Thursday	**Friday**	**Saturday**	**Sunday**
jueves	viernes	sábado	domingo
HWEH-vehs	*V'YEHR-nehs*	*SA-ba-doh*	*doh-MEEN-go*

next Monday	**last Tuesday**	**on Fridays**
el lunes próximo	el martes pasado	los viernes
el LOO-nehs PROHX-see-mo	*el MAR-tehs pa-SA-doh*	*lohs V'YEHR-nehs*

January	**February**	**March**
enero	febrero	marzo
eh-NEH-ro	*feh-BREH-ro*	*MAR-so*

April	**May**	**June**
abril	mayo	junio
ah-BREEL	*MA-yo*	*HOON-yo*

July	**August**	**September**
julio	agosto	septiembre
HOOL-yo	*ah-GOHS-toh*	*sep-T'YEM-breh*

October	**November**	**December**
octubre	noviembre	diciembre
ohk-TOO-breh	*no-V'YEM-breh*	*dee-S'YEM-breh*

On what date?
¿En qué fecha?
¿en keh FEH-cha?

March 1st
El primero de marzo
*el pree-MEH-ro deh
MAR-so*

the 2nd	**the 3rd**	**the 4th**	etc.
el dos	el tres	el cuatro	
el dohs	*el trehs*	*el KWA-tro*	

The 25th of December
El veinticinco de diciembre
*el VAIN-tee-SEEN-ko deh
dee-S'YEM-breh*

Merry Christmas!
¡Feliz Navidad!
¡feh-LEES nah-vee-DAHD!

The 1st of January
El primero de enero
*el pree-MEH-ro deh
eh-NEH-ro*

Happy New Year!
¡Feliz Año Nuevo!
*¡feh-LEES AHN-yo
NWEH-vo!*

Independence Day
El día de la Independencia
*el DEE-ah deh la een-deh-
pen-DEN-s'ya*

Long live _____!
¡Viva _____!
¡VEE-va _____!

A propósito: Spanish countries have different national holidays and many religious ones. The feast day of a particular
saint is called la fiesta de San (or Santa) . . . followed by
the saint's name. Such holidays vary according to country
or city and are generally colorful and interesting to see.

7. Money

Some Spanish-speaking countries use pesos with different values according to the country. Spain uses pesetas, and other countries give the peso a variety of names, sometimes taken from the names of national heroes—the bolívar in Venezuela, the boliviano in Bolivia, the balboa in Panama, the sucre in Ecuador—and sometimes from ancient Indian tradition, like the sol (sun) in Peru and the quetzal (a sacred bird) in Guatemala.

Where can I change money?
¿Dónde puedo cambiar dinero?
¿DOHN-deh PWEH-doh kahm-B'YAR dee-NEH-ro?

Can I change dollars here?
¿Puedo cambiar dólares aquí?
¿PWEH-doh kahm-B'YAR DOH-la-rehs ah-KEE?

Where is a bank?
¿Dónde hay un banco?
¿DOHN-deh I oon BAHN-ko?

What time does the bank open?
¿A qué hora abre el banco?
¿ah keh OH-ra AH-breh el BAHN-ko?

What time does the bank close?
¿A qué hora cierra el banco?
¿ah keh OH-ra S'YEH-rra el BAHN-ko?

What's the dollar rate?
¿A cómo está el cambio del dólar?
¿ah KO-mo ess-TA el KAHM-b'yo del DOH-lar?

Twelve pesos for one dollar.
Doce pesos por un dólar.
DOH-seh PEH-sohs por oon DOH-lar.

I want to change $50.
Quiero cambiar cincuenta dólares.
K'YEH-ro kahm-B'YAR seen-KWEN-ta DOH-la-rehs.

Do you accept traveler's checks?
¿Aceptan cheques de viajero?
¿ah-SEP-tahn CHEH-kehs deh v'ya-HEH-ro?

Of course.
Desde luego.
DEHS-deh L'WEH-go.

Not here.
Aquí no.
ah-KEE no.

Will you accept a personal check?
¿Aceptan un cheque personal?
¿ah-SEP-tahn oon CHEH-keh pehr-so-NAHL?

Have you identification?
¿Tiene Ud. identificación?
¿T'YEH-neh oo-STED ee-den-tee-fee-ka-S'YOHN?

Yes, here is my passport.
Sí, aquí está mi pasaporte.
see, ah-KEE ess-TA mee pa-sa-POR-teh.

Give me two 100-peso notes.
Deme dos billetes de a cien pesos.
DEH-meh dohs beel-YEH-tehs deh ah s'yen PEH-sohs.

. . . ten 50-peso notes.
. . . diez billetes de a
cincuenta.
*. . . d'yess beel-YEH-tehs
deh ah seen-KWEN-ta.*

. . . five 20-peso notes.
. . . cinco billetes de a
veinte.
*. . . SEEN-ko beel-YEH-
tehs deh ah VAIN-teh.*

I need some small change.
Necesito cambio.
neh-seh-SEE-toh KAHM-b'yo.

8. Basic Foods

The foods and drinks mentioned in this section will enable you to be well fed in any Spanish-speaking country. The section that follows this will deal with special regional dishes of Spain and Latin America that you will encounter in your travels.

breakfast
desayuno
des-ah-YOO-no

orange juice
jugo de naranja
HOO-go deh na-RAHN-ha

grapefruit
toronja
toh-ROHN-ha

soft-boiled eggs
huevos pasados por agua
WEH-vohs pa-SA-dohs por AH-gwa

fried eggs
huevos fritos
WEH-vohs FREE-tohs

an omelet
una tortilla de huevos
OO-na tor-TEEL-ya deh WEH-vohs

scrambled eggs
huevos revueltos
WEH-vohs rev-WEL-tohs

with bacon
con tocino
kohn toh-SEE-no

with ham
con jamón
kohn ha-MOHN

toast
tostadas
tohs-TA-dahs

coffee with hot milk
café con leche
ka-FEH kohn LEH-cheh

marmalade
mermelada
mehr-meh-LA-da

black coffee
café negro
ka-FEH NEH-gro

with cream
con crema
kohn KREH-ma

with sugar
con azúcar
kohn ah-SOO-kahr

cocoa	tea	with lemon
chocolate	té	con limón
cho-ko-LA-teh	*teh*	*kohn lee-MOHN*

lunch	dinner
almuerzo	cena
ahl-MWEHR-so	*SEH-na*

Do you know a good restaurant?
¿Conoce Ud. un buen restaurante?
¿ko-NO-seh oo-STED oon bwehn rest-ow-RAHN-teh?

A table for three.	This way, please
Una mesa para tres.	Por aquí, por favor.
OO-na MEH-sa PA-ra	*por ah-KEE, por fa-VOR.*
··trehs.	

The menu, please.	What's good?
El menú, por favor.	¿Qué hay de bueno?
el meh-NOO, por fa-VOR.	*¿keh I deh BWEH-no?*

What do you recommend?	What is it?
¿Qué recomienda Ud.?	¿Qué es?
¿keh re-ko-M'YEN-da	*¿keh ess?*
oo-STED?	

Good.	I'll try it.	Give me this.
Bueno.	Lo probaré.	Déme esto.
BWEH-no.	*lo pro-ba-REH.*	*DEH-meh*
		ESS-toh.

First a cocktail.
Primero un coctel.
pree-MEH-ro oon kohk-TEHL.

soup	fish	oysters
sopa	pescado	ostras
SO-pa	*pes-KA-doh*	*OHS-trahs*

shrimps
camarones
ka-ma-RO-nehs

lobster
langosta
lahn-GOHS-ta

roasted	**broiled**	**fried**	**boiled**
asado	a la parrilla	frito	hervido
ah-SA-doh	*ah la pa-* *REEL-ya*	*FREE-toh*	*ehr-VEE-doh*

roast chicken	**fried chicken**	**turkey**	**duck**
pollo asado	pollo frito	pavo	pato
POHL-yo ah- *SA-doh*	*POHL-yo* *FREE-toh*	*PA-vo*	*PA-toh*

roast pork
lechón asado
leh-CHOHN ah-SA-doh

pork chops
chuletas de cerdo
choo-LEH-tahs deh SEHR-doh

veal chops
chuletas de ternera
choo-LEH-tahs deh ter-NEH-ra

lamb chops
chuletas de cordero
choo-LEH-tahs deh kor-DEH-ro

roast lamb
cordero asado
kor-DEH-ro ah-SA-doh

beef
carne de res
KAR-neh deh ress

steak
bistec
bees-TEK

well done
bien cocido
b'yen ko-SEE-doh

medium
término medio
TEHR-mee-no MEH-d'yo

rare
poco cocido
PO-ko ko-SEE-doh

hamburger	**bread**	**butter**
hamburguesa	pan	mantequilla
am-boor-GEH-sa	*pahn*	*mahn-teh-KEEL-ya*

potatoes (Latin America)	**potatoes (Spain)**	**fried potatoes**
papas	patatas	papas fritas
PA-pahs	*pa-TA-tahs*	*PA-pahs FREE-tahs*

noodles	**rice**	**vegetables**	**green beans**
fideos	arroz	legumbres	habichuelas
fee-DEH-ohs	*ah-RROHS*	*leh-GOOM-bress*	*ah-bee-CHWEH-lahs*

peas (Spain)	**peas (Latin America)**	**carrots**
guisantes	petit pois	zanahorias
ghee-SAHN-tess	*peh-tee PWA*	*sa-na-OHR-yahs*

spinach	**cabbage**	**onions**	**mushrooms**
espinaca	repollo	cebollas	setas
ess-pee-NA-ka	*reh-POHL-yo*	*seh-BOHL-yahs*	*SEH-tahs*

asparagus	**salad**	**oil**	**vinegar**
espárrago	ensalada	aceite	vinagre
ess-PA-rra-go	*en-sa-LA-da*	*ah-SAY-teh*	*vee-NA-greh*

salt	**pepper**
sal·	pimienta
sahl	*pee-M'YEN-ta*

What wine do you recommend?
¿Qué vino recomienda?
¿keh VEE-no reh-ko-M'YEN-da?

white wine	**red wine**
vino blanco	vino tinto
VEE-no BLAHN-ko	*VEE-no TEEN-toh*

beer	**champagne**	**To your health!**
cerveza	champaña	¡A su salud!
sehr-VEH-sa	*chahm-PAHN-ya*	*¡ah soo sa-LOOD!*

fruits	**grapes**	**peaches**	**apples**
frutas	uvas	melocotones	manzanas
FROO-tahs	*OO-vahs*	*me-lo-ko-TOH-nehs*	*mahn-SA-nahs*

pears	**bananas**	**pineapples**
peras	bananas	piñas
PEH-rahs	*ba-NA-nahs*	*PEEN-yahs*

strawberries	**oranges**
fresas	naranjas
FREH-sahs	*na-RAHN-hahs*

a dessert	**pastry**	**cake**
un postre	pastelería	torta
oon POHS-treh	*pas-teh-leh-REE-ya*	*TOR-ta*

ice cream	**cheese**
helado	queso
eh-LA-doh	*KEH-so*

coffee	**demitasse**
café	café solo
ka-FEH	*ka-FEH SO-lo*

More, please.
Más, por favor.
mahs, por fa-VOR.

That's enough, thank you.
Suficiente, gracias.
soo-fee-S'YEN-teh, GRA-s'yahs.

Waiter!   Waitress!
¡Camarero!   ¡Camarera!
¡ka-ma-REH-ro!   *¡ka-ma-REH-ra!*

The check, please.
La cuenta, por favor.
la KWEN-ta, por fa-VOR.

Is the tip included?
¿Está incluída la propina?
¿ess-TA een-kloo-EE-da la pro-PEE-na?

I think the bill is incorrect.
Creo que la cuenta está incorrecta.
KREH-oh keh la KWEN-ta ess-TA een-ko-RREK-ta.

Oh no, sir.   Look here.   You see?
Oh no, señor.   Mire aquí.   ¿Ve Ud.?
oh no, sen-YOR.   *MEE-reh ah-*   *¿veh oo-STED?*
                     KEE.

Yes, it's true.   It's O.K.
Sí, es verdad.   Está bien.
see, ess ver-DAHD.   *ess-TA b'yen.*

Come again soon.
Vuelva pronto.
VWEL-va PROHN-toh.

Point to the Answer

Sírvase indicar en esta página su contestación a mi pregunta. Muchas gracias.
Please point on this page to your answer to my question. Thank you very much.

Esta es nuestra specialidad.
This is our specialty.

Está listo.
It's ready.

No está listo.
It isn't ready.

Se necesita un cuarto de hora.
It takes a quarter of an hour.

Esto se sirve sólo los viernes.
That is served only on Fridays.

Es pollo, cerdo, cordero, ternera, res, pescado, mariscos.
It's chicken, pork, lamb, veal, beef, fish, seafood.

... con legumbres.
... with vegetables.

... con salsa.
... with a sauce.

9. Food Specialties of the Spanish World

These expressions and names of dishes will be useful in restaurants or private homes where you may be invited. These dishes commonly appear on most Spanish or Latin American menus and are so much a part of Spanish and Latin American dining tradition that you should recognize them and know how to pronounce them as well as to enjoy them! We have written the Spanish names first, since that is how you will see it on the menu.

What is today's special?
¿Cuál es el plato del día?
¿kwahl ess el PLA-toh del DEE-ya?

Is it ready?
¿Está listo?
¿ess-TA LEES-toh?

How long will it take?
¿Cuánto tiempo demora?
¿KWAHN-toh T'YEM-po deh-MO-ra?

Gazpacho andaluz
gahs-PA-cho ahn-da-LOOSS
Cold soup of raw onions, cucumber, tomatoes, garlic, oil, and vinegar

Caldo gallego
KAHL-doh ghal-YEH-go
Soup of meat and vegetables

Puchero
poo-CHEH-ro
Thick soup of meat, corn, and other vegetables

Calamares en su tinta
ka-la-MA-rehs en soo TEEN-ta
Squids cooked in their black juice

Bacalao a la vizcaína
ba-kahl-OW ah la vees-ka-EE-na
Salt codfish with onions, peppers, and tomato sauce

Filetes de lenguado empanados
fee-LEH-tehs deh len-GWA-doh em-pa-NA-dohs
Breaded fillet of sole

Zarzuela
sar-SWEH-la
Assorted shellfish, stewed

Fabada
fa-BA-da
Stew of sausage, pork, bacon, and beans

Arroz con pollo
ah-RROHS kohn POHL-yo
Chicken steamed with rice, onions, tomatoes, and saffron

Paella valenciana
pa-EL-ya va-len-S'YA-na
Chicken, sausage, mussels, clams, lobster, peppers, onions,
    tomatoes, and saffron rice

Pollo en cazuela
POHL-yo en ka-SWEH-la
Stew of chicken and vegetables

Lechón asado
le-CHOHN ah-SA-doh
Roast suckling pig

Ropa vieja
RO-pa V'YEH-ha
Braised beef with tomato and pimiento sauce

Picadillo
pee-ka-DEEL-yo
Chopped beef and pork steamed with tomatoes, onions, and peppers

Mole de guajalote
MO-leh deh gwa-ha-LO-teh
Turkey with sauce of bitter chocolate and hot peppers

Enchiladas
en-chee-LA-dahs
Cornmeal pancakes filled with meat and chili sauce, raw onions, and grated cheese

Moros y cristianos ("Moors and Christians")
MO-rohs ee kreess-T'YA-nohs
Black beans, rice, diced ham, peppers, tomatoes, and garlic

Huevos rancheros
WEH-vohs ran-CHEH-rohs
Fried eggs with chili sauce, raw onion, grated cheese, and tortillas

Jamón serrano
ha-MOHN seh-RRA-no
Thin-sliced smoked ham

Guacamole
gwa-ka-MO-leh
Avocado mashed with hot peppers, onions, tomatoes, lime juice, and garlic

Flan
flahn
Caramel custard

Cascos de guayaba con queso
KAHS-kohs deh gwa-YA-ba kohn KEH-so
Preserved guava with cream cheese

How do you like it?
¿Cómo le parece?
¿KO-mo leh pa-REH-seh?

It's delicious!
¡Está delicioso!
¡ess-TA deh-lee-S'YO-so!

It's very tasty!
¡Está riquísimo!
¡ess-TA ree-KEE-see-mo!

My congratulations to the cook (male)!
¡Mis felicitaciones al cocinero!
¡mees feh-lee-see-ta-S'YO-nehs ahl ko-see-NEH-ro!

. . . to the cook (female)!
. . . a la cocinera!
. . . ah la ko-see-NEH-ra!

Thank you for a wonderful dinner!
¡Mil gracias por una cena exquisita!
¡meel GRA-s'yahs por OO-na SEH-na es-kee-SEE-ta!

You are welcome.
Por nada.
por NA-da.

I'm happy that you enjoyed it.
Encantado que le haya gustado.
en-kahn-TA-doh keh leh AH-ya goo-STA-doh.

10. Transportation

Getting around by public transportation is enjoyable not only for the new and interesting things you see, but also because of the opportunities you have for practicing Spanish. To make your travels easier, use short phrases when speaking to drivers or others when you ask directions. And don't forget **Por favor** and **Gracias!**

Bus

Where is the bus stop?
¿Dónde está la parada de autobús?
¿DOHN-deh ess-TA la pa-RA-da deh ow-toh-BOOSS?

Do you go to the Plaza Mayor?
¿Ud. va a la Plaza Mayor?
¿oo-STED va ah la PLA-sa ma-YOR?

No, take number nine.
No, tome el número nueve.
no, TOH-meh el NOO-meh-ro NWEH-veh.

How much is the fare?
¿Cuánto es el pasaje?
¿KWAHN-toh ess el pa-SA-heh?

Where do you want to go?
¿Adónde quiere ir?
¿ah-DOHN-deh K'YEH-reh eer?

To the cathedral.
A la catedral.
ah la ka-teh-DRAHL.

Is it far?
¿Está lejos?
¿ess-TA LEH-hohs?

No, it's near.
No, está cerca.
no, ess-TA SEHR-ka.

Please tell me where to get off.
Dígame, por favor, dónde debo bajar.
DEE-ga-meh, por ja-VOR, DOHN-deh DEH-bo ba-HAR.

Get off here.
Baje aquí.
BA-heh ah-KEE.

Point to the Answer

Sírvase indicar en esta página su contestación a mi pre-
gunta. Muchas gracias.
Please point on this page to your answer to my question.
Thank you very much.

Allá.
Over there.

Por allá.
That way.

En la esquina.
At the corner.

En el otro lado de la calle.
On the other side of the
street.

A la derecha.
To the right.

A la izquierda.
To the left.

Derecho.
Straight ahead.

No sé.
I don't know.

Taxi

Taxi.
Taxi.
TAHX-see.

Are you free?
¿Está libre?
¿ess-TA LEE-breh?

Where to?
¿Adónde vamos?
¡ah-DOHN-deh VA-mohs?

To this address.
A esta dirección.
ah ESS-ta dee-rek-S'YOHN.

Do you know where it is?
¿Sabe dónde está?
*¿SA-beh DOHN-deh
ess-TA?*

I am in a hurry.
Tengo prisa.
TEN-go PREE-sa.

Go faster!
¡Vaya más rápido!
¡VA-ya mahs RAHP-ee-doh!

Slower!
¡Más despacio!
¡mahs dess-PA-s'yo!

Stop here.
Pare aquí.
PA-reh ah-KEE.

At the corner.
En la esquina.
En la ess-KEE-na.

Wait for me.
Espéreme.
ess-PEH-reh-meh.

One can't park here.
Aquí no se puede estacio-
nar.
*ah-KEE no seh PWEH-deh
ess-tá-s'yo-NAR.*

I'll be back soon.
Volveré pronto.
vohl-veh-REH PROHN-toh.

In five minutes.
En cinco minutos.
en SEEN-ko mee-NOO-tohs.

O.K., I'll wait for you.
Está bien, le espero.
ess-TA b'yen, leh ess-PEH-ro.

How much is it by the hour?
¿Cuánto es por hora?
¿KWAHN-toh ess por OH-ra?

. . . **per kilometer?**
. . . por kilómetro?
. . . por kee-LO-meh-tro?

Call for me tomorrow.
Venga mañana a buscarme.
VEN-ga mahn-YA-na ah boo-SKAR-meh.

In the morning.	**In the afternoon.**
Por la mañana.	Por la tarde.
por la mahn-YA-na.	*por la TAR-deh.*

At 3 o'clock.	**At the hotel** _____.
A las tres.	En el hotel _____.
ah lahs trehs.	*en el o-TEL* _____.

A propósito: Tip 10% of the meter but for longer trips make arrangements *before* you start. Some cities have taxis that operate along a specified street like small buses and charge a nominal sum to each of the various passengers they pick up. This is a good way to cut down on taxi fares as well as to improve your Spanish.

Point to the Answer

Sírvase indicar en esta página su contestación a mi pregunta. Muchas gracias.
Please point on this page to your answer to my question. Thank you very much.

Le esperaré aquí.
I'll wait for you here.

No puedo esperar.
I can't wait.

Volveré para buscarlo.
I'll be back to pick you up.

No es suficiente.	**El equipaje es extra.**
It's not enough.	The baggage is extra.

Train and Subway

Is there a subway in this city?
¿Hay subterráneo en esta ciudad?
¿I soob-teh-RRA-neh-o en ESS-ta s'yoo-DAHD?

Where is the subway?
¿Dónde está el subterráneo?
¿DOHN-deh ess-TA el soob-teh-RRA-neh-yo?

Where is the railroad station?
¿Dónde está la estación de ferrocarriles?
¿DOHN-deh ess-TA la ess-ta-S'YOHN deh feh-rro-ka-RREEL-lehs?

Where do I buy the tickets?
¿Dónde se compran los billetes?
¿DOHN-deh seh KOHM-prahn lohs beel-YEH-tess?

One ticket for Granada.
Un billete para Granada.
oon beel-YEH-teh PA-ra gra-NA-da:.

Round trip.
Ida y vuelta.
EE-da ee VWEL-ta.

One way only.
Ida solamente.
EE-da so-la-MEN-teh.

First class.
Primera clase.
pree-MEH-ra KLA-seh.

Second class.
Segunda clase.
seh-GOON-da KLA-seh.

A timetable.
Un itinerario.
oon ee-tee-neh-RA-r'yo.

Where is the train for Santiago?
¿Dónde está el tren para Santiago?
¿DOHN-deh ess-TA el trehn PA-ra sahn-T'YA-go?

On what platform is the train?
¿En que andén está el tren?
¿en keh ahn-DEHN ess-TA el trehn?

When do we leave?
¿Cuándo salimos?
¿KWAHN-doh sa-LEE-mohs?

Is this seat taken?
¿Está ocupado este asiento?
¿ess-TA oh-koo-PA-doh ESS-teh ah-S'YEN-toh?

With your permission, madam.
Con permiso, señora.
kohn per-MEE-so, sen-YO-ra.

Of course, sir.
Como no, señor.
KO-mo no, sen-YOR.

At what time do we get to Veracruz?
¿A qué hora llegamos a Veracruz?
¿ah keh OH-ra l'yeh-GA-mohs ah veh-ra-KROOSS?

Does the train stop in Puebla?
¿Se para el tren en Puebla?
¿seh PA-ra el trehn en PWEH-bla?

How long are we stopping here?
¿Cuánto tiempo demoramos aquí?
¿KWAHN-toh T'YEM-po deh-mo-RA-mohs ah-KEE?

Where is the dining car?
¿Dónde está el coche comedor?
¿DOHN-deh ess-TA el KO-cheh ko-meh-DOR?

I can't find my ticket.
No puedo encontrar mi billete.
no PWEH-doh en-kohn-TRAR mee beel-YEH-teh.

Wait!
¡Espere!
¡ess-PEH-reh!

Here it is!
¡Aquí está!
¡ah-KEE ess-TA!

Prepare my berth, please.
Prepare mi camarote, por favor.
preh-PA-reh mee ka-ma-RO-teh, por fa-VOR.

Can you help me?
¿Puede ayudarme?
¿PWEH-deh ah-yoo-DAR-meh?

I took the wrong train.
Tomé el tren equivocado.
toh-MEH el trehn eh-kee-vo-KA-doh.

I want to go to ———.
Quiero ir a ———.
K'YEH-ro eer ah ———.

Point to the Answer

Sírvase indicar en esta página su contestación a mi pregunta. Muchas gracias.
Please point on this page to your answer to my question. Thank you very much.

La vía número ———.
Track number ———.

Por allí.
That way.

Abajo.
Downstairs.

Arriba.
Upstairs.

Éste no es el tren suyo.
This is not your train.

Debe cambiar de tren en ———.
You must change trains at ———.

Sale en ——— minutos.   **Llegamos a las ———.**
It leaves in ——— minutes.   We arrive at ——— o'clock.

Ship

To the dock.
Al muelle.
ahl MWEHL-yeh.

Can one go on board now?
¿Se puede ir a bordo ahora?
¿seh PWEH-deh eer ah BOR-doh ah-OH-ra?

At what time does the ship sail?
¿A qué hora zarpa el barco?
¿ah keh OH-ra SAR-pa el BAR-ko?

I feel seasick.
Me siento mareado. (m) . . . mareada. (f)
meh S'YEN-toh ma-reh-AH-doh. . . . ma-reh-AH-da.

Does the boat stop in La Guaira?
¿Para el barco en La Guaira?
¿PA-ra el BAR-ko en la G'WY-ra?

11. Traveling by Automobile

Car Rental

Where can one rent a car?
¿Dónde se puede alquilar un auto?
¿DOHN-deh seh PWEH-deh ahl-kee-LAR oon OW-toh?

. . . a motorcycle?
. . . una motocicleta?
. . . OO-na mo-toh-see-KLEH-ta?

. . . a bicycle?
. . . una bicicleta?
. . . OO-na bee-see-KLEH-ta?

I want to rent a car.
Quiero alquilar un auto.
K'YEH-ro ahl-kee-LAR oon OW-toh.

How much per day?
¿Cuánto cuesta por día?
¿KWAHN-toh KWESS-ta por DEE-ya?

How much per kilometer?
¿Cuánto cuesta por kilómetro?
¿KWAHN-toh KWESS-ta por kee-LO-meh-tro?

Is the gasoline included?
¿Está incluída la gasolina?
¿ess-TA een-kloo-EE-da la ga-so-LEE-na?

Is the transmission automatic?
¿Es de cambio automático?
¿ess deh KAHM-b'yo ow-toh-MA-tee-ko?

I would like to try it out.
Me gustaría probarlo.
meh goo-sta-REE-ya pro-BAR-lo.

A propósito: The word for "car" is **coche** in Spain, and **carro** in Latin America. In Spain **carro** means "cart," while in Latin America **coche** means "coach." "Automobile" is **automóvil** or **auto** in all Spanish-speaking countries.

Distances are reckoned in kilometers, approximately ⅝ of a mile.

Gas Station

Where can one buy gasoline?
¿Dónde se puede comprar gasolina?
¿DOHN-deh seh PWEH-deh kohm-PRAR ga-so-LEE-na?

How much per liter?*
¿Cuánto es por litro?
¿KWAHN-toh ess por LEE-tro?
* Gas is sold by the liter (1.05 quarts). In other words, four liters is about one gallon.

Thirty liters, please.	**Fill it up.**
Treinta litros, por favor.	Llénelo.
TRAIN-ta LEE-trohs, por fa-VOR.	*L'YEH-neh-lo.*

Please . . . put air in the tires.
Por favor . . . ponga aire en las llantas.
por fa-VOR . . . PON-ga I-reh en lahs L'YAHN-tahs.

Look at the water.	**. . . the battery.**
Vea el agua.	. . . la batería.
VEH-ah el AH-gwa.	*. . . la ba-teh-REE-ya.*
. . . the oil.	**. . . the spark plugs.**
. . . el aceite.	. . . las bujías.
. . . el ah-SAY-teh.	*. . . lahs boo-HEE-yahs.*
. . . the brakes.	**. . . the carburetor.**
. . . los frenos.	. . . el carburador.
. . . lohs FREH-nohs.	*. . . el kar-boo-ra-DOR.*

Change the oil.
Cambie el aceite.
KAHM-b'yeh el ah- SAY-teh.

Grease the motor.
Engrase el motor.
en-GRA-seh el mo-TOR.

Change this tire.
Cambie esta llanta.
*KAHM-b'yeh ESS-ta
L'YAHN-ta.*

Wash the car.
Lave el auto.
LA-veh el OW-toh.

A road map, please.
Un mapa de carreteras, por
favor.
*oon MA-pa deh ka-rreh-
TEH-rahs, por fa-VOR.*

Where are the restrooms?
¿Dónde están los lavabos?
¿DOHN-deh ess-TAHN los la-VA-bohs?

Asking Directions

Where does this road go to?
¿Adónde va esta carretera?
¿ah-DOHN-deh ESS-ta ka-rreh-TEH-ra?

Is this the way to Mérida?
¿Es éste el camino para Mérida?
¿ess ESS-teh el ka-MEE-no PA-ra MEH-ree-da?

Is the road good?
¿Está bueno el camino?
¿ess-TA BWEH-no el ka-MEE-no?

Which is the road to San José?
¿Cuál es la vía para San José?
¿kwahl ess la VEE-ya PA-ra sahn ho-SEH?

It's that way.
Es por allí.
ess por ahl-YEE.

Is the next town far?
¿Está lejos el próximo pueblo?
¿ess-TA LEH-hohs el PROHX-see-mo PWEH-blo?

Do you know if there is a good restaurant there?
¿Sabe Ud. si hay un buen restaurante allí?
¿SA-beh oo-STED see I oon bwehn rest-ow-RAHN-teh ahl-YEE?

Is there a good hotel in Arequipa?
¿Hay un buen hotel en Arequipa?
¿I oon bwehn o-TEL en ah-reh-KEE-pa?

Yes, there is a very good one.
Sí, hay uno muy bueno.
see, I OO-no mwee BWEH-no.

Good enough.
Bastante bueno.
bahs-TAHN-teh BWEH-no.

Is it far?
¿Está lejos?
¿ess-TA LEH-hohs?

I don't know.
No sé.
no seh.

About ——— kilometers.
Unos ——— kilómetros.
OO-nohs ——— kee-LO-meh-trohs.

Follow this road.
Siga por esta carretera.
SEE-ga por ESS-ta ka-rreh-TEH-ra.

Turn right . . .
Doble a la derecha . . .
DOH-bleh ah la deh-REH-cha . . .

. . . as you leave the village.
. . . al salir del pueblo.
. . . ahl sa-LEER del PWEH-blo.

When you come to the bridge . . .
Cuando llegue al puente . . .
KWAHN-doh L'YEH-geh ahl PWEN-teh . . .

. . . cross . . .
. . . cruce . . .
. . . KROO-seh . . .

. . . and turn left.
. . . y doble a la izquierda.
. . . ee DOH-bleh ah la ees-K'YEHR-da.

Go straight ahead.
Siga derecho.
SEE-ga deh-REH-cho.

The road is not bad.
El camino no está malo.
el ka-MEE-no no ess-TA MA-lo.

But . . . take the expressway.
Pero . . . tome la autopista.
PEH-ro . . . TOH-meh la ow-toh-PEESS-ta.

Point to the Answer

Sírvase indicar en esta página su contestación a mi pre
   gunta. Muchas gracias.
Please point on this page to your answer to my question
   Thank you very much.

Tome a la derecha. Turn right.	Tome a la izquierda. Turn left.
Siga derecho. Go straight ahead.	hasta . . . until . . .

En la próxima luz roja . . .
At the next red light . . .

Ud. está en este punto en este mapa.
You are at this point on this map.

Siga este camino.
Follow this road.

El próximo pueblo se llama ————.
The next town is called ————.

Emergencies and Repairs

Your license!
¡Su licencia!
¡soo lee-SEN-s'ya!

Here it is, officer.
Aquí está, señor agente.
ah-KEE ess-TA, sen-YOR ah-HEN-teh.

And the registration.
Y la matrícula.
ee la ma-TREE-koo-la.

It wasn't my fault.
No fue culpa mía.
no fweh KOOL-pa MEE-ah.

The truck skidded.
El camión patinó.
el ka-mee-OHN pa-tee-NO.

This imbecile crashed into me.
Este imbécil me chocó.
ESS-teh eem-BEH-seel meh cho-KO.

A propósito: As the Spanish drive with considerable dash and challenge, **imbécil, idiota,** and **bruto** are frequent and even rather mild expletives. However, control and good humor, plus a diplomatic use of Spanish, will make car travel safe and very enjoyable.

I am in trouble.
Estoy en un apuro.
ess-TOY en oon ah-POO-ro.

My car has broken down.
Mi coche se ha descom-
    puesto.
*mee KO-cheh seh ah
    des-kohm-PWESS-toh.*

Could you help me?
¿Podría ayudarme?
*¿po-DREE-ya ah-yoo-
    DAR-meh?*

I have a flat tire.
Tengo una llanta pinchada.
*TEN-go OO-na L'YAHN-
    ta peen-CHA-da.*

Can you lend me a jack?
¿Puede prestarme un gato?
*¿PWEH-deh press-TAR-
    meh oon GA-toh?*

It's stuck.
Está atascado.
ess-TA ah-tahs-KA-doh.

Can you push me?
¿Puede empujarme?
*¿PWEH-deh em-poo-
    HAR-meh?*

A thousand thanks!
¡Mil gracias!
meel GRA-s'yahs!

You are very kind.
Es usted muy amable.
ess oo-STED mwee ah-MA-bleh.

I want to see the mechanic.
Quiero ver al mecánico.
K'YEH-ro vehr ahl meh-KA-nee-ko.

He doesn't work on weekends.
No trabaja los fines de semana.
no tra-BA-ha los FEE-nehs deh seh-MA-na.

What's the matter?
¿Qué pasa?
¿keh PA-sa?

The car doesn't go well.
El coche no anda bien.
el KO-cheh no AHN-da b'yen.

There is a funny noise in the motor.
Hay un ruido raro en el motor.
I oon RWEE-doh RA-ro en el mo-TOR.

It's difficult to start.
Arranca con dificultad.
ah-RAHN-ka kohn dee-fee-kool-TAHD

Can you fix it?
¿Puede arreglarlo?
¿PWEH-deh ah-rreh-GLAR-lo?

What will it cost?
¿Cuánto costará?
¿KWAHN-toh kohs-ta-RA?

How long will it take?
¿Cuánto tiempo tomará?
¿KWAHN-toh T'YEM-po toh-ma-RA?

Today it isn't possible.
Hoy no es posible.
oy no ess po-SEE-bleh.

Perhaps tomorrow.
Quizá mañana.
kee-SA mahn-YA-na.

When will it be ready?
¿Cuándo estará listo?
¿KWAHN-doh ess-ta-RA LEES-toh?

In two hours.
En dos horas.
en dohs OH-rahs.

A propósito: For making sure exactly when the car will be ready, consult the phrases in the "Time" section, page 32.

Point to the Answer

Sírvase indicar en esta página su contestación a mi pregunta. Muchas gracias.
Please point on this page to your answer to my question. Many thanks.

Esto le saldrá a ——— pesos.
It will cost you ——— pesos.

Estará listo en ——— horas.
It will be ready in ——— hours.

Mañana.
Tomorrow.

Pasado mañana.
The day after tomorrow.

No tenemos la pieza.
We don't have the part.

Podemos repararlo temporariamente.
We can repair it temporarily.

International Road Signs

Danger

Caution

Sharp turn

Crossroads

Right curve

Left curve

**Guarded RR
crossing**

**Unguarded RR
crossing**

Bumps

Main road ahead

One way

Do not enter

No parking

Parking

In addition you will hear or see the following instructions:

GUARDE SU DERECHA
GWAHR-deh soo deh-
  REH-cha
Keep to the right

DESVÍO
des-VEE-yo
Detour

UNA VÍA
OO-na VEE-ya
One way

ENCRUCIJADA
Enn-kroo-see-HA-da
Crossroads

VELOCIDAD MÁXIMA —— KM.
veh-lo-see-DAHD MAHX-ee-ma —— kee-LO-
  meh-trohs
Maximum speed —— kilometers

SE PROHIBE
  ESTACIONAR
seh pro-EE-beh ess-ta-
  s'yo-NAR
No parking

CURVA
KOOR-va
Curve

OBRAS EN PROGRESO
OH-brahs en pro-GREH-so
Work in progress

REDUZCA LA
  VELOCIDAD
re-DOOS-ka la veh-lo-
  see-DAHD
Reduce speed

ENTRADA
en-TRA-da
Entrance

SALIDA
sa-LEE-da
Exit

PROHIBIDO EL PASO A BICICLETAS
pro-ee-BEE-doh el PA-so ah bee-see-KLEH-tahs
No bicycles

PEATONES
peh-ah-TOH-nehs
Pedestrians

12. Sightseeing and Photography

We have combined these two important sections since you will want to take pictures of what you are seeing. If you are taking pictures indoors, be sure to ask the custodian ¿Está permitido?—"Is it permitted?"

Sightseeing

I need a guide.
Necesito un guía.
neh-seh-SEE-toh oon GHEE-ya.

Are you a guide?
¿Es Ud. guía?
¿ess oo-STED GHEE-ya?

Do you speak English?
¿Habla Ud. inglés?
¿AH-bla oo-STED een-GLEHS?

It doesn't matter.
No importa.
no eem-POR-ta.

I speak a little Spanish.
Hablo un poco de español.
AH-blo oon PO-ko de ess-pahn-YOHL.

Do you have a car?
¿Tiene auto?
¿TYEH-neh OW-toh?

How much do you charge per hour?
¿Cuánto cobra por hora?
¿KWAHN-toh KO-bra por OH-ra?

How much per day?
¿Cuánto por día?
¿KWAHN-toh por DEE-ya?

For two people?
¿Para dos personas?
¿PA-ra dohs pehr-SO-nahs?

A group of four?
¿Un grupo de cuatro?
¿oon GROO-po deh KWA-tro?

We would like to see the old part of the city.
Nos gustaría ver la parte antigua de la ciudad.
*nohs goo-sta-REE-ya vehr la PAR-teh ahn-TEE-gwa deh
la s'yoo-DAHD.*

Where is the Plaza de Toros?
¿Dónde queda la Plaza de Toros?
¿DOHN-deh KEH-da la PLA-sa deh TOH-rohs?

We want to go . . .   **. . . to the Prado Museum.**
Queremos ir . . .   . . . al Museo del Prado.
keh-REH-mohs eer . . .   *. . . ahl moo-SEH-oh del
                                       PRA-doh.*

. . . to the Plaza San Martín.
. . . a la plaza San Martín.
. . . a la PLA-sa sahn mar-TEEN.

. . . to the central park.
. . . al parque central.
. . . ahl PAHR-keh sen-TRAHL.

. . . to the zoo.
. . . al jardín zoológico.
. . . ahl har-DEEN so-oh-LO-hee-ko.

. . . to the San Juan market.
. . . al mercado de San Juan.
. . . ahl mehr-KA-doh deh sahn hwahn.

. . . to see the archaeological excavations.
. . . a ver las excavaciones arqueológicas.
*. . . a vehr lahs ex-ka-vah-S'YO-nehs ar-keh-oh-LO-
hee-kahs.*

. . . to the royal palace.
. . . al palacio real.
. . . ahl pa-LA-s'yo reh-AHL.

How beautiful!
¡Qué bello!
¡keh BEL-yo!

Very interesting!
¡Muy interesante!
¡mwee een-teh-reh-SAHN-teh!

From what period is this?
¿De qué época es esto?
¿deh keh EH-po-ka ess ESS-toh?

Do you know a good nightclub?
¿Conoce un buen club nocturno?
¿ko-NO-seh oon bwehn kloob nohk-TOOR-no?

Let's go.
Vamos.
VA-mohs.

You are a very good guide.
Es Ud. un guía muy bueno.
ess oo-STED oon GHEE-ya mwee BWEH-no.

Come again tomorrow.
Vuelva mañana.
VWEL-va mahn-YA-na.

At 9 o'clock.
A las nueve.
ah lahs NWEH-veh.

And, if you don't have a guide:

May one enter?
¿Se puede entrar?
¿seh PWEH-deh
   en-TRAR?

It is open.
Está abierto.
ess-TA ah-B'YEHR-toh.

It is closed.
Está cerrado.
ess-TA sehr-RA-doh.

What are the visiting hours?
¿Cuáles son las horas de visita?
¿KWAH-lehs sohn lahs OH-rahs deh vee-SEE-ta?

It opens at 2 o'clock.
Abre a las dos.
AH-breh ah lahs dohs.

It is closed for repairs.
Está cerrado por reparaciones.
ess-TA seh-RRA-doh por reh-pa-ra-S'YO-nehs.

Can one take photos?
¿Se puede tomar fotografías?
¿seh PWEH-deh toh-MAR fo-toh-gra-FEE-yahs?

It is permitted.   **It is forbidden.**
Está permitido.   Está prohibido.
ess-TA pehr-mee-TEE-doh.   *ess-TA pro-ee-BEE-doh.*

Leave your packages in the checkroom.
Deje sus paquetes en el guardarropa.
DEH-heh soos pa-KEH-tehs en el gwahr-da-RRO-pa.

What is the admission?
¿Cuánto cuesta la entrada?
¿KWAHN-toh KWES-ta la en-TRA-da?

The admission is free.
La entrada es gratis.
la en-TRA-da ess GRA-teess.

Two pesos 50 centavos.   **And, for children?**
Dos pesetas cincuenta.   Y, ¿para niños?
dohs peh-SEH-tahs seen-   *ee, ¿PA-ra NEEN-yohs?*
KWEN-ta.

Your ticket, please.   **Follow me.**
Su billete, por favor.   Sígame.
soo beel-YEH-teh, por   *SEE-ga-meh.*
fa-VOR.

No smoking.   **This way, please.**
Prohibido fumar.   Por aquí, por favor.
Pro-ee-BEE-doh foo-MAR.   *por ah-KEE, por fa-VOR.*

This castle . . .
Este castillo . . .
ESS-teh kahs-TEEL-yo . . .

This palace . . .
Este palacio . . .
ESS-teh pa-LA-s'yo . . .

This church . . .
Esta iglesia . . .
ESS-ta ee-GLEH-s'ya . . .

This monument . . .
Este monumento . . .
ESS-teh mo-noo-MEN-
toh . . .

This street . . .
Esta calle . . .
ESS-ta KAHL-yeh . . .

This square . . .
Esta plaza . . .
ESS-ta PLA-sa . . .

What is it called?
¿Cómo se llama?
¿KO-mo seh l'ya-ma?

It's magnificent!
¡Es magnífico!
¡ess mahg-NEE-fee-kol

It's very interesting!
¡Es muy interesante!
¡es mwee een-teh-reh-SAHN-teh!

It's very old, isn't it?
Es muy antiguo, ¿verdad?
ess mwee ahn-TEE-gwo, ¿vehr-DAHD?

This is for you.
.Esto es para Ud.
ESS-toh ess PA-ra oo-STED.

Some signs you may see in public places:

CABALLEROS	or	HOMBRES	DAMAS
ka-bahl-YEH-rohs		*OHM-brehs*	*DA-mahs*
Gentlemen		Men	Ladies

ENTRADA	SALIDA	ABIERTO	CERRADO
en-TRA-da	*sa-LEE-da*	*ah-B'YEHR-*	*şeh-RRA-*
Entrance	Exit	*toh*	*doh*
		Open	Closed

HORAS DE VISITA
OH-rahs deh vee-SEE-ta
Visiting hours

INFORMA-CIÓN
• een-for-ma-S'YOHN
Information

VESTUARIO
ves-TWA-r'yo
Checkroom

CALIENTE
ka-L'YEN-teh
Hot

FRÍO
FREE-yo
Cold

TIRE
TEE-reh
Pull

EMPUJE
em-POO-heh
Push

SE PROHIBE ENTRAR
seh pro-EE-beh en-TRAR
No admittance

SE PROHIBE FUMAR
seh pro-EE-beh foo-MAR
No smoking

ESTÁ PROHIBIDO FIJAR CARTELES
ess-TA pro-ee-BEE-doh fee-HAR kar-TEH-lehs
No sign posting

A propósito: The term **prohibido** or **se prohibe** in signs has the general connotation of "No" or "Don't do it"; so when you see these words, don't walk on the grass, smoke, take photographs, or whatever the case may be.

Photography

Where is a camera shop?
¿Dónde hay una tienda de efectos de fotografía?
¿DOHN-deh I OO-na T'YEN-da deh eh-FEK-tohs deh fo-toh-gra-FEE-ya?

I would like a roll of film
Quisiera un rollo
kee-S'YEH-ra oon ROHL-yo

. . . in color.
. . . en colores.
. . . en ko-LO-rehs.

... black and white.
... blanco y negro.
... *BLAHN-ko ee NEH-gro.*.

... movie film.
... una película.
... *OO-na peh-LEE-koo-la.*

For this camera.
Para esta cámara.
PA-ra ESS-ta KA-ma-ra.

This is to be developed.
Esto es para revelar.
ESS-to ess PA-ra reh-veh-LAR.

How much, per print?
¿Cuánto cuesta cada fotografía?
¿KWAHN-to KWEHS-ta KA-da fo-toh-gra-FEE-ya?

Two of each.
Dos de cada una.
dohs deh KA-da OO-na.

An enlargement.
Una ampliación.
OO-na ahm-plee-ya-S'YOHN.

About this size.
Más o menos de este tamaño.
mahs oh MEH-nohs deh ESS-teh ta-MAHN-yo.

When will they be ready?
¿Cuándo estarán listas?
¿KWAHN-do ess-ta-RAHN LEES-tahs?

May I take a photograph of you?
¿Puedo tomar una foto de Ud.?
¿PWEH-doh toh-MAR OO-na FO-toh deh oo-STED?

Stand here.
Párese aquí.
PA-reh-seh ah-KEE.

Don't move.
No se mueva.
no seh MWEH-va.

Smile.
Sonría.
sohn-REE-ya.

That's it.
Así es.
ah-SEE ess.

Will you kindly take one of me?
¿Me quiere sacar una foto a mí?
¿meh K'YEH-reh sa-KAR OO-na FO-toh ah mee?

In front of this.
Delante de esto.
deh-LAHN-teh deh ESS-toh.

You are very kind.
Es Ud. muy amable.
ess oo-STED mwee ah-MA-bleh.

May I send you a copy?
¿Le puedo mandar una copia?
¿leh PWEH-doh mahn-DAR OO-na KOHP-ya?

Your name?   **Your address?**
¿Su nombre?   ¿Su dirección?
¿soo NOHM-breh?   *¿soo dee-rek-S'YOHN?*

A propósito: Asking to take pictures of someone often leads to more general conversation, For this reason the following three sections will be especially interesting to you.

Point to the Answer

Sírvase indicar en esta página su contestación a mi pregunta. Muchas gracias.
Please point on this page to your answer to my question. Thank you very much.

Venga mañana.   A las ———.
Come tomorrow   At ——— o'clock.

Vuelva en —— días.
Come back in —— days.

Podemos repararlo.   No podemos repararlo.
We can repair it.   We cannot repair it.

No tenemos.
We haven't any.

13. Entertainment

This section will show you how to extend and accept invitations, as well as suggest things to do. It also offers some typical conversations for theater or nightclubs and some suitable words of appreciation when you are asked for dinner.

Things to Do

May I invite you ...
¿Puedo invitarle ...
¿PWEH-doh een-vee-TAR-leh ...

... to dinner?
... a cenar?
... ah seh-NAR?

... to go for a drive?
... a dar una vuelta en auto?
... ah dar OO-na VWEL-ta en OW-toh?

... to play bridge?
... a jugar al bridge?
... ah hoo-GAR ahl bridge?

... to the theater?
... al teatro?
... ahl teh-AH-tro?

... to play tennis?
... a jugar al tenis?
... ah hoo-GAR ahl TEH-nees?

... to lunch?
... a almorzar?
... ah ahl-mor-SAR?

... to have a drink?
... a tomar algo?
... ah toh-MAR AHL-go?

... to dance?
... a bailar?
... ah by-LAR?

... to the movies?
... al cine?
... ahl SEE-neh?

... to play golf?
... a jugar golf?
... ah hoo-GAR golf?

Thank you very much.
Muchas gracias.
MOO-chahs GRA-s'yahs.

With pleasure.
Con mucho
gusto.
kohn MOO-cho
GOO-sto.

I am sorry.
Lo siento.
lo S'YEN-toh.

I cannot.
No puedo.
no PWEH-doh.

I am busy.
Estoy ocupado. (m)
ess-TOY oh-koo-PA-doh.
Estoy ocupada. (f)
ess-TOY oh-koo-PA-da.

I am tired.
Estoy cansado. (m)
ess-TOY kahn-SA-doh.
Estoy cansada. (f)
ess-TOY kahn-SA-da.

I'm waiting for someone.
Estoy esperando a alguien.
ess-TOY ess-peh-RAHN-doh ah AHL-g'yen.

I don't feel well.
No me siento bien.
no meh S'YEN-toh b'yen.

Another time, perhaps.
Una otra vez, quizá.
OO-na OH-tra vess, kee-SA.

Where are we going tomorrow?
¿Adónde vamos mañana?
¿ah-DOHN-deh VA-mohs mahn-YA-na?

Let's go . . .
Vamos . . .
VA-mohs . . .

. . . take a walk around town.
. . . a dar una vuelta por la ciudad.
. . . ah dar OO-na VWEL-ta por
la s'yoo-DAHD.

. . . to the art museum.
. . . al museo de arte.
. . . ahl moo-SEH-oh deh
AR-teh.

. . . to the central market.
. . . al mercado central.
. . . ahl mer-KA-doh'
sen-TRAHL.

. . . to the cathedral.
. . . a la catedral.
. . . ah la ka-teh-DRAHL.

. . . to the palace.
. . . al palacio.
. . . ahl pa-LA-s'yo.

... to the shops.
... a las tiendas.
... *ah lahs TYEN-dahs.*

... to the park.
... al parque.
... *ahl PAR-keh.*

... to see the national
dances.
... a ver los bailes
nacionales.
... *ah vehr lohs BY-lehs
na-s'yo-NA-lehs.*

... to the beach.
... a la playa.
... *ah la PLA-ya.*

... to the soccer game.
... al partido de fútbol.
... *ahl par-TEE-doh deh
FOOT-bohl.*

... to a discoteque.
... a una discoteca.
... *ah OO-na dees-ko
TEH-ka.*

... to the bullfight.
... a la corrida de toros.
... *ah la ko-RREE-da deh
TOH-rohs.*

... to a typical restaurant.
... a un restaurante típico.
... *ah oon rest-ow-
RAHN-teh TEE-pee-ko.*

... to the zoo.
... al zoológico.
... *ahl so-oh-LO-hee-ko.*

... to the meeting.
... a la reunión.
... *ah la reh-oo-N'YOHN.*

... to the races.
... a las carreras.
... *ah lahs ka-RREH-rahs.*

Who's ahead?
¿Quién está ganando?
*¿k'yen ess-TA
ga-NAHN-doh?*

... to the movies.
... al cine.
... *ahl SEE-neh.*

Bravo!
¡Ole!
¡OH-leh!

A propósito: Bullfighting, popular in the majority of Spanish countries, has its own vocabulary, such as: the team

—cuadrilla; the pointed darts—banderillas; the horsemen
—picadores; and the main bullfighter—el matador ("the
one who kills"). All participants are called toreros. The
word toreador is *never* used. Bullfight tickets are sold
for the sombra (shade) or sol (sun) side of the bullring.
When you go, be sure to ask for una entrada de sombra—
"a ticket in the shade."

Theater and Nightclubs

Let's go to the theater.
Vamos al teatro.
VA-mohs ahl teh-AH-tro.

Two seats, please.
Dos localidades, por favor.
dohs lo-ka-lee-DA-dehss, por fa-VOR.

In the orchestra.
En platea.
en pla-TEH-ah.

In the balcony.
En el balcón.
en el bahl-KOHN

How beautiful she is!
¡Qué bella es!
¡keh BEL-ya ess!

Who is playing the lead?
¿Quién hace el papel principal?
¿k'yen AH-seh el pa-PEL preen-see-PAHL?

When does it start?
¿Cuándo comienza?
¿KWAHN-doh ko-M'YEN-sa?

What do you think of it?
¿Qué le parece?
¿keh leh pa-REH-seh?

It's very good.
Es muy bueno.
ess mwee BWEH-no.

It's great.
Es fantástico.
ess fahn-TAHS-tee-ko.

It's very amusing.
Es muy divertido.
ess mwee dee-vehr-TEE-doh.

Is it over?
¿Terminó?
¿tehr-mee-NO?

Let's go to a nightclub.
Vamos a un cabaret.
VA-mohs ah oon ka-ba-REH.

A table near the dance floor.
Une mesa cerca de la pista.
OO-na MEH-sa SEHR-ka deh la PEES-ta.

Is there a minimum charge?
¿Hay un mínimo?
¿I oon MEE-nee-mo?

Shall we stay?
¿Nos quedamos?
¿nohs keh-DA-mohs?

Shall we dance?
¿Bailamos?
¿by-LA-mohs ?

Let's leave.
Vámonos.
VA-mo-nohs.

An Invitation to Dinner

Can you come for dinner at our house, Monday at eight?
¿Puede venir a cenar a casa el lunes a las ocho?
*¿PWEH-deh veh-NEER ah seh-NAR ah KA-sa el
   LOO-nehs ah lahs OH-cho?*

With pleasure.
Con mucho gusto.
kohn MOO-cho GOO-sto.

**If it isn't inconvenient for
   you.**
Si no es mucha molestia
   para Ud.
*See no ess MOO-cha mo-
   LES-t'ya PA-ra oo-STED.*

Very happy to see you.
Mucho gusto en verle.
*MOO-cho GOO-sto en
   VEHR-leh.*

Sorry I'm late.
Siento llegar tarde.
*S'YEN-toh l'yeh-GAR
   TAR-deh.*

The traffic was terrible.
El tránsito estaba terrible.
el TRAHN-see-toh ess-TA-ba teh-RREE-bleh.

Make yourself at home.
Está Ud. en su casa.
ess-TA oo-STED en soo KA-sa.

What a beautiful house!
¡Qué casa tan bella!
¡keh KA-sa tahn BEL-ya!

Will you have something to drink?
¿Quiere algo de beber?
¿K'YEH-reh AHL-go deh beh-BEHR?

A cigarette?
¿Un cigarillo?
¿oon see-ga-RREEL-yo?

To your health!
¡A su salud!
¡ah soo sa-LOOD!

Dinner is served.
La cena está servida.
la SEH-na ess-TA sehr-VEE-da.

Will you sit here, please?
¿Quiere sentarse aquí, por favor?
¿K'YEH-reh sen-TAR-seh ah-KEE, por fa-VOR?

What a delicious meal!
¡Qué comida tan deliciosa!
¡keh ko-MEE-da tahn deh-lee-S'YO-sa!

But have some more!
¡Pero sírvase más!
¡PEH-ro SEER-va-seh mahs!

We had a wonderful time.
Nos divertimos mucho.
nohs dee-vehr-TEE-mohs MOO-cho.

We must go.
Tenemos que irnos.
teh-NEH-mohs keh EER-nohs.

What a shame!
¡Qué lástima!
¡keh LAHS-tee-ma!

I'll drive you back.
Yo los llevo en el auto.
yo lohs L'YEH-vo en el OW-toh.

No, please don't bother.
No, por favor, no se moleste.
no, por fa-VOR, no seh mo-LESS-teh.

Many thanks for your hospitality.
Muchísimas gracias por su hospitalidad.
moo-CHEE-see-mahs GRA-s'yahs por soo ohs-pee-ta-
  lee-DAHD.

Until soon.
Hasta pronto.
AHS-ta PROHN-toh.

14. Talking to People

Most phrase books are too preoccupied with attending to one's wants and generally "getting along" to pay much attention to what you should say once you meet someone, such as asking people about themselves, their families, and even their opinions about things. Use of the short phrases in this section, both the questions and the answers, can lead to a rewarding conversational breakthrough in Spanish.

Do you live in this city?
¿Vive Ud. en esta ciudad?
¿VEE-veh oo-STED en ESS-ta s'yoo-DAHD?

Where are you from?
¿De dónde es Ud.?
¿deh DOHN-deh ess oo-STED?

I am from Barcelona.
Soy de Barcelona.
soy deh bar-seh-LO-na.

Really?
¿Verdad?
¿vehr-DAHD?

It's a beautiful city.
Es una hermosa ciudad.
ess OO-na ehr-MO-sa s'yoo-DAHD.

I've been there.
He estado allí.
eh ess-TA-doh ahl-YEE.

I would like to go there.
Me gustaría ir allí.
meh goo-sta-REE-ya eer ahl-YEE.

How long have you been here?
¿Hace cuánto tiempo está aquí?
¿AH-seh KWAHN-toh T'YEM-po ess-TA ah-KEE?

For three days.
Hace tres días.
AH-seh trehs DEE-yahs.

Several weeks.
Varias semanas.
VA-r'yahs seh-MA-nahs.

Two months.
Dos meses.
dohs MEH-sehs.

How long will you stay here?
¿Cuánto tiempo va a quedarse aquí?
¿KWAHN-toh T'YEM-po va ah keh-DAR-seh ah-KEE?

I will stay ———.
Me quedaré ———.
meh keh-da-REH ———.

Have you been here before?
¿Ha estado aquí antes?
*¿ah ess-TA-doh ah-KEE
  AHN-tehs?*

No, never,
No, nunca.
no, NOON-ka.

Once.
Una vez.
OO-na vess.

Five years ago.
Hace cinco años.
*AH-seh SEEN-ko
  AHN-yohs.*

Where are you living?
¿Dónde vive Ud.?
*¿DOHN-deh VEE-veh
  oo-STED?*

At what hotel?
¿En qué hotel?
¿en keh o-TEL?

What do you think of Sevilla?
¿Qué le parece Sevilla?
¿keh leh pa-REH-seh seh-VEEL-ya?

I like it very much.
Me gusta mucho.
meh GOO-sta MOO-cho.

It's very interesting.
Es muy interesante.
*ess mwee een-teh-reh-
  SAHN-teh.*

The city is beautiful.
La ciudad es hermosa.
*la s'yoo-DAHD ess
  ehr-MO-sa.*

**The women are very
  beautiful.**
Las mujeres son muy
  hermosas.
*las moo-HEH-rehs son
  mwee ehr-MO-sahs.*

Have you been in Granada?
¿Ha estado Ud. en Granada?
¿ah ess-TA-doh oo-STED en gra-NA-da?

You must go there.
Tiene que ir allá.
T'YEH-neh keh eer ahl-YA.

Are you from the United States?
¿Es Ud. de los Estados Unidos?
¿ess oo-STED deh lohs ess-TA-dohs oo-NEE-dohs?

Yes, I am from San Francisco.
Sí, soy de San Francisco.
see, soy deh sahn frahn-SEES-ko.

I speak a little Spanish.
Hablo un poquito de español.
AH-blo oon po-KEE-toh deh ess-pahn-YOHL.

But you have a good accent.
Pero Ud. tiene un buen acento.
PEH-ro oo-STED T'YEH-neh oon bwehn ah-SEN-toh.

You are very kind.
Es Ud. muy amable.
ess oo-STED mwee ah-MA-bleh.

Have you been in the United States?
¿Ha estado en los Estados Unidos?
¿ah ess-TA-doh en lohs ess-TA-dohs oo-NEE-dohs?

Where have you been?
¿Dónde ha estado?
¿DOHN-deh ah ess-TA-doh?

What do you think of ———?
¿Qué piensa de ———?
¿keh P'YEN-sa deh ———?

Do you like ———?
¿Le gusta ———?
¿leh GOO-sta ———?

When people ask your opinion about something, you will find the following comments most helpful.

Very interesting.
Muy interesante.
mwee een-teh-reh-SAHN-teh.

Not bad.
No está mal.
no ess-TA mahl.

Magnificent.
Magnífico.
mahg-NEE-fee-ko.

Wonderful.
Maravilloso.
ma-ra-veel-YO-so.

Sometimes.
Algunas veces.
ahl-GOO-nahs VEH-sehs.

Often.
A menudo.
ah meh-NOO-doh.

Never.
Nunca.
NOON-ka.

It seems to me that . . .
Me parece que . . .
meh pa-REH-seh keh . . .

In any case . . .
En todo caso . . .
en TOH-doh KA-so . . .

It's a shame!
¡Es una lástima!
¡ess OO-na LAHS-tee-ma!

I agree with you.
Estoy de acuerdo.
ess-TOY deh ah-KWER-doh.

I don't know.
No sé.
no seh.

I have forgotten.
He olvidado.
eh ohl-vee-DA-doh.

Is it possible?
¿Es posible?
¿ess po-SEE-bleh?

That's true.
Es verdad.
ess vehr-DAHD.

You must come to see us.
Debe Ud. venir a vernos.
DEH-beh oo-STED veh-
  NEER ah VEHR-nohs.

At our house.
En nuestra casa.
en NWESS-tra KA-sa.

It would be a great pleasure.
Sería un gran placer.
seh-REE-ya oon grahn pla-SEHR.

Are you married?
¿Es Ud. casado? (m)
¿ess oo-STED ka-SA-doh?

¿Es Ud. casada? (f)
¿ess oo-STED ka-SA-da?

I am not married.
Soy soltero. (m)
soy sohl-TEH-ro.
Soy soltera. (f)
soy sohl-TEH-ra.

I am married.
Soy casado. (m)
soy ka-SA-doh.
Soy casada. (f)
soy ka-SA-da.

Is your wife (husband) here?
¿Está aquí su esposa (esposo)?
¿ess-TA ah-KEE soo ess-PO-sa (ess-PO-so)?

Yes, over there.
Sí, allá.
see, ahl-YA.

Do you have children?
Tiene niños?
T'YEH-neh NEEN-yohs?

No, I haven't.
No, no tengo.
no, no TEN-go.

Yes, I have.
Sí, tengo.
see, TEN-go.

How many boys?
¿Cuántos niños?
¿KWAHN-tohs NEEN-yohs?

How many girls?
¿Cuántas niñas?
¿KWAHN-tahs NEEN-yahs?

How old are they?
¿Qué edad tienen?
¿keh eh-DAHD T'YEH-nen?

My son is seven years old.
Mi hijo tiene siete años.
mee EE-ho T'YEH-neh S'YEH-teh AHN-yohs.

My daughter is ten years old.	**What cute children!**
Mi hija tiene diez años.	¡Qué niños tan monos!
mee EE-ha T'YEH-neh d'yess AHN-yohs.	*¡keh NEEN-yohs tahn MO-nohs!*

This is my . . .	**. . . mother.**	**. . . sister.**
Ésta es mi . . .	. . . madre.	. . . hermana.
ESS-ta ess mee . . .	*. . . MA-dreh.*	*. . . ehr-MA-na.*

. . . wife.	**. . . daughter.**
. . . esposa.	. . . hija.
. . . ess-PO-sa.	*. . . EE-ha.*

. . . daughter-in-law.	**. . . granddaughter.**
. . . nuera.	. . . nieta.
. . . NWEH-ra.	*. . . N'YEH-ta.*

This is my . . .	**. . . father.**	**. . . brother.**
Éste es mi . . .	. . . padre.	. . . hermano.
ESS-teh ess mee . . .	*. . . PA-dreh.*	*. . . ehr-MA-no.*

. . . husband.	**. . . son.**
. . . esposo.	. . . hijo.
. . . ess-PO-so.	*. . . EE-ho.*

. . . son-in-law.	**. . . grandson.**
. . . yerno.	. . . nieto.
. . . YEHR-no.	*. . . N'YEH-to.*

For "your," "his," or "her" use su in place of mi—"my."

Do you know . . .	**. . . that man?**	**. . . that lady?**
Conoce Ud. a . . .	. . . ese hombre?	. . . esa señora?
ko-NO-seh oo-	*. . . ESS-seh*	*. . . ESS-sa*
STED ah . . .	*OHM-breh?*	*sen-YO-ra?*

. . . **Mrs. Martin?**
. . . la señora de Martín?
. . . la sen-YO-ra deh mar-TEEN?

He is . . .	**. . . a writer.**
Él es . . .	. . . escritor.
el ess . . .	*. . . ess-kree-TOR.*

. . . **a business man.**
. . . hombre de negocios.
. . . OHM-breh deh neh-GO-s'yohs.

. . . a lawyer.	**. . . a manu-**	**. . . a doctor.**
. . . abogado.	**facturer.**	. . . doctor.
. . . ah-bo-	. . . fabricante.	*. . . dohk-TOR.*
GA-doh.	*. . . fa-bree-*	
	KAHN-teh.	

. . . a banker.	**. . . a military**	**. . . a painter.**
. . . banquero.	**man.**	. . . pintor.
. . . bahn-	. . . militar.	*. . . peen-TOR.*
KEH-ro.	*. . . mee-lee-TAR.*	

. . . a professor.	**. . . a politician.**	**. . . an actor.**
. . . profesor.	. . . político.	. . . actor.
. . . pro-feh-	*. . . po-LEE-*	*. . . ahk-TOR.*
SOR.	*tee-ko.*	

. . . **a member of the government.**
. . . miembro del gobierno.
. . . M'YEM-bro del go-B'YEHR-no.

She is . . .	**. . . a writer.**
Ella es . . .	. . . escritora.
EL-ya ess . . .	*. . . ess-kree-TOH-ra.*

. . . a singer.	**. . . an actress.**	**. . . a teacher.**
. . . cantante.	. . . actriz.	. . . maestra.
. . . kahn-TAHN-teh.	*. . . ahk-TREESS.*	*. . . ma-ESS-tra.*

And for other masculine endings in -*or*, add -*a* for a woman.

I don't know.	**I'll find out.**
No sé.	Averiguaré.
no seh.	*ah-veh-ree-gwa-REH.*

He is Spanish.	**She is Spanish.**
Él es español.	Ella es española.
el ess ess-pahn-YOHL.	*EL-ya ess ess-pahn-YO-la.*

He is Mexican.	**She is Mexican.**
Él es mexicano.	Ella es mexicana.
el ess meh-hee-KA-no.	*EL-ya ess meh-hee-KA-na.*

He is North American.	**She is North American.**
(from the U.S.)	Ella es norteamericana.
Él es norteamericano.	*EL-ya ess nor-teh-*
el ess nor-teh-	*ah-meh-ree-KA-na.*
ah-meh-ree-KA-no.	

He is English.	**She is English.**
El es inglés.	Ella es inglesa.
el ess een-GLEHSS.	*EL-ya ess een-GLEH-sa.*

A propósito: For nationalities of Spanish-speaking and other important countries, see the dictionary section.

He is very nice.	**She is very nice.**
Él es muy simpático.	Ella es muy simpática.
el ess mwee seem-PA-tee-ko.	*EL-ya ess mwee seem-PA-tee-ka.*

She is very pretty.
Ella es muy bonita.
EL-ya ess mwee bo-NEE-ta.

He (she) is very intelligent.
Él (ella) es muy inteligente.
*el (EL-ya) ess mwee
een-teh-lee-HEN-teh.*

He (she) is very capable.
Él (ella) es muy capaz.
*el (EL-ya) ess mwee
ka-PAHS.*

Here is my address.
Aquí está mi dirección.
*ah-KEE ess-TA mee
dee-rek-S'YOHN.*

What is your address?
¿Cuál es su dirreción?
¿kwahl ess soo dee-rek-S'YOHN?

Here is my telephone number.
Aquí está mi número de teléfono.
ah-KEE ess-TA mee NOO-meh-ro deh teh-LEH-fo-no.

**What is your telephone
number?**
¿Cuál es su número de
teléfono?
*¿kwahl ess soo NOO-meh-ro
deh teh-LEH-fo-no?*

May I call you?
¿Puedo llamarle?
¿PWEH-doh l'ya-MAR-leh?

When?
¿Cuándo?
¿KWAHN-doh?.

Tomorrow morning.'
Mañana por la mañana.
mahn-YA-na por la mahn-YA-na.

Early.
Temprano.
tem-PRA-no.

In the afternoon.
Por la tarde.
por la TAR-deh.

What is your first name?
¿Cuál es su primer nombre?
*¿kwahl ess soo pree-MEHR
NOHM-breh?*

Mine is Richard.
El mío es Ricardo.
el MEE-yo ess ree-KAR-do.

You dance very well.
Ud. baila muy bien.
*oo-STED BY-la mwee
b'yen.*

You sing very well.
Ud. canta muy bien.
*oo-STED KAHN-ta mwee
b'yen.*

What a pretty dress!
¡Qué vestido tan bonito!
¡keh ves-TEE-doh tahn bo-NEE-toh!

I have a surprise for you.
Tengo una sorpresa para Ud.
*TEN-go OO-na sor-PREH-sa
PA-ra oo-STED.*

Do you like it?
¿Le gusta?
¿leh GOOS-ta?

Can we see each other again?
¿Podemos volver a vernos?
¿po-DEH-mohs vohl-VEHR ah VEHR-nohs?

When?
¿Cuándo?
¿KWAHN-doh?

Where?
¿Dónde?
¿DOHN-deh?

What's the matter?
¿Qué le pasa?
¿keh leh PA-sa?

Are you angry?
¿Está enojado? (to a man)
¿ess-TA· eh-no-HA-doh?

¿Está enojada? (to a woman)
¿ess-TA eh-no-HA-da?

Why?
¿Por qué?
¿por keh?

Where are you going?
¿A dónde va?
¿ah DOHN-deh va?

Let's go together.
Vamos juntos.
VA-mohs HOON-tohs.

You are intelligent.
Ud. es inteligente.
oo-STED ess een-teh-lee-HEN-teh.

You are very beautiful.
Ud. es muy hermosa. (f)
oo-STED ess mwee ehr-MO-sa.

You are very nice.
Ud. es muy simpática. (f)
oo-STED ess mwee seem-PA-tee-ka.

Will you give me your photograph?
¿Me da una foto de Ud.?
¿meh da OO-na FO-toh deh oo-STED?

Will you write to me?   **Don't forget.**
¿Me escribirá?   No se olvide.
¿meh ess-kree-bee-RA?   *no seh ohl-VEE-deh.*

I like you very much.
Yo te quiero mucho.
yo teh K'YEH-ro MOO-cho.

Really?
¿De verdad?
¿deh vehr-DAHD?

Do you like me too?
¿Me quieres a mí también?
¿meh K'YEH-rehs ah mee tahm-B'YEN?

I love you.
Te quiero.
teh K'YEH-ro.

A propósito: In the last sentences we have used the familiar form for "you," both in the verb and the pronoun, since the tone of the conversation implies a certain degree of familiarity.

"To like," "to love," and "to want" are all expressed by the same verb—querer.

15. Words That Show You Are "With It"

There are certain words that Spanish-speaking people use constantly but that do not always have an exact equivalent in English. To use them at the right time will cause Spanish people to consider not only that you have a diploma in good manners but that you have an excellent foundation in Spanish culture patterns—in other words, that you are "with it." The Spanish is given first, just as you will hear these expressions occur in everyday conversation.

We have divided these words into two groups; the first one is composed of selected polite expressions:

¡Buen viaje!
¡bwehn V'YA-heh!
Have a good trip!

¡Que se divierta!
¡keh seh dee-V'YEHR-ta!
Enjoy yourself!

¡Que lo pase bien!
¡keh lo PA-seh b'yen!
Have a nice time!

¡Felicitaciones!
¡feh-lee-see-ta-S'YO-nehs!
Congratulations!

Mis saludos a . . .
mees sa-LOO-dohs ah . . .
My regards to . . .

¡A su salud!
¡ah soo sa-LOOD!
To your health!

When you see someone eating you say:

¡Buen provecho! or ¡Que aproveche!
¡bwehn pro-VEH-cho! ¡keh ah-pro-VEH-cheh!
Good benefit! May you enjoy it!

When someone sneezes you say:

¡Salud! or ¡Jesús!
¡sa-LOOD! ¡heh-SOOS!
Health! Jesus!

When someone leaves the room or passes in front of someone, he says:

Con permiso.
kohn pehr-MEE-so.
With permission.

To which the answer is:

¿Cómo no?
¿KO-mo no?
How (why) not?

To a visitor to your house you say:

¡Está en su casa!
¡ess-TA en soo KA-sa!
Make yourself at home! (You are in your house!)

To someone who admires something of yours:

Es suyo. or Es suya.
ess SOO-yo; ess SOO-ya.
It is yours.

(Use suyo if the thing is masculine, suya if it is feminine.)

A propósito: In general be careful about admiring small objects, because the reply Es suyo sometimes means that it will literally be given to you. It is better to admire the house or the garden, and the reply Es suya or Está a su disposición means that it is yours to enjoy (but not to take away).

As the following phrases permeate conversation, it will interest you to know what they mean, as well as to learn to use them as helpful conversational stopgaps. The translations are quite free as these expressions are very idiomatic.

¡Claro!	Pues . . .	Entonces . . .
¡KLA-ro!	*pwehss . . .*	*en-TOHN-*
Of course!	So . . .	*sehs . . .*
		Then, so . . .

Bueno . . .
BWEH-no . . .
Well . . .

No me diga.
no meh DEE-ga.
You don't say . . .

¿Qué pasa?
¿keh PA-sa?
What's happening?

¿Qué tal?
¿keh tahl?
How goes it?

Así, así.
ah-SEE, ah-SEE.
So, so.

¿No es verdad?
¿no ess vehr-
    DAHD?
Isn't it so?

¡Qué raro!
¡keh RA-ro!
How strange!

¡Qué va!
¡keh va!
Not at all!

No se preocupe.
no seh preh-oh-
    KOO-peh.
Don't worry.

Vamos a ver.
VA-mohs ah
    vehr.
Let's see.

No es nada.
no ess NA-da.
It's nothing.

No importa.
no eem-POR-ta.
It doesn't matter.

Lo mismo da.
lo MEES-mo da.
It's all the same.

No vale la pena.
no VA-leh la PEH-na.
It isn't worthwhile.

Más o menos.
mahs oh MEH-
    nohs.
More or less.

En todo caso . . .
en TO-doh
    KA-so . . .
In any case . . .

Cualquier cosa.
kwahl-K'YEHR
    KO-sa.
Anything.

¡Fíjese!
¡FEE-heh-seh!
Just imagine!

¡Ni hablar!
¡nee ah-BLAR!
Don't mention it!

¿Qué hay?
¿keh I?
What's up?

Parece mentira.
pa-REH-seh men-TEE-ra.
It seems a lie (impossible).

¿Cómo dice?
¿KO-mo DEE-seh?
What's that? or How's that?

¡Caramba!
¡ka-RAHM-ba!
Good Heavens! Well, really! For Heaven's sake!

No faltaba más.
no fahl-TA-ba mahs.
That's all we needed.

¡Eso es!
¡ES-so ess!
That's it!

¡Dios mío!
¡d'yohs MEE-yo!
My God! (Great heavens!)

¡Ave María!
¡AH-veh ma-REE-ya!
Hail Mary! (Great heavens!)

¡Hombre!	¡Mujer!	¡Chico!	¡Chica!
¡OHM-breh!	*¡moo-HEHR!*	*¡CHEE-ko!*	*¡CHEE-ka!*
Man!	Woman!	Boy!	Girl!

A propósito: The last four words are used colloquially to
give emphasis or punctuation to what you are saying.
¡Hombre! is the most widely used, sometimes even by
women talking to each other.

16. Shopping

Shops in Spain and Latin America still tend to be specialized although there exist chains of general stores and even the supermarket—**supermercado.**

Names of Shops

Where can one find . . .
¿Dónde se puede encontrar . . .
¿*DOHN-deh seh PWEH-deh en-kohn-TRAR* . . .

. . . a department store?
. . . una tienda de departamentos?
. . . *OO-na T'YEN-da deh deh-par-ta-MEN-tohs?*

. . . a dress shop?
. . . una tienda de vestidos?
. . . *OO-na T'YEN-da deh ves-TEE-dohs?*

. . . a hat shop?
. . . una sombrerería?
. . . *OO-na som-breh-reh-REE-ya?*

. . . a perfume shop?
. . . una perfumería?
. . . *OO-na per-joo-meh-REE-ya?*

. . . a jewelry shop?
. . . una joyería?
. . . *OO-na ho-yeh-REE-ya?*

. . . a drugstore?
. . . una farmacia?
. . . *OO-na far-MA-s'ya?*

. . . a book shop?
. . . una librería?
. . . *OO-na lee-breh-REE-ya?*

. . . a toy shop?
. . . una juguetería?
. . . *OO-na hoo-geh-teh-REE-ya?*

. . . an antique shop?
. . . una tienda de antigüedades?
. . . *OO-na T'YEN-da deh ahn-tee-gweh-DA-dehs?*

... **a shoe store?**
... una zapatería?
... *OO-na sa-pa-teh-REE-ya?*

... **a flower shop?**
... una floristería?
... *OO-na flo-rees-teh-REE-ya?*

... **a camera shop?**
... una tienda para artículos de fotografía?
... *OO-na T'YEN-da PA-ra ar-TEE-koo-lohs de fo-toh-gra-FEE-ya?*

... **a tobacco shop?**
... una tabaquería?
... *OO-na ta-ba-keh-REE-ya?*

... **a beauty shop?**
... un salón de belleza?
... *oon sa-LOHN deh behl-YEH-sa?*

... **a barber shop?**
... una barbería?
... *OO-na bar-beh-REE-ya?*

... **a grocery store?**
... una casa de comestibles?
... *OO-na KA-sa deh ko-mehs-TEE-blehs?*

... **a market?**
... un mercado?
... *oon mehr-KA-doh?*

A propósito: A **mercado** is also a general market place and, in Latin America, is often held in the plaza of small towns and villages on certain days each week.

General Shopping Vocabulary

May I help you?
¿En qué puedo servirle?
*¿en keh PWEH-doh
sehr-VEER-leh?*

What do you wish?
¿Qué desea?
¿keh deh-SEH-ah?

I would like to buy . . .
Me gustaría comprar . . .
*meh goo-sta-REE-ya
kohm-PRAR . . .*

. . . a gift for my husband.
. . . un regalo para mi
esposo.
*. . . oon reh-GA-lo PA-ra
mee es-PO-so.*

. . . a gift for my wife.
. . . un regalo para mi señora.
. . . oon reh-GA-lo PA-ra mee sen-YO-ra.

. . . something for a man.
. . . algo para un hombre.
. . . AHL-go PA-ra oon OHM-breh.

. . . something for a lady.
. . . algo para una dama.
. . . AHL-go PA-ra OO-na DA-ma.

Nothing for the moment.
Nada por el momento.
NA-da por el mo-MEN-toh.

I'm just looking around.
Estoy mirando solamente.
es-TOY mee-RAHN-doh so-la-MEN-teh.

I'll be back later.
Regreso más tarde.
reh-GREH-so mahs TAR-deh.

I like this.
Me gusta esto.
meh GOO-sta ESS-toh.

... that.
... eso.
... ES-so.

How much is it?
¿Cuánto es?
¿KWAHN-toh ess?

Show me another.
Muéstreme otro.
MWEHS-treh-meh OH-tro.

Something less expensive.
Algo menos caro.
AHL-go MEH-nohs KA-ro.

Do you like this?
¿Le gusta esto?
¿leh GOO-sta ESS-toh?

Is it handmade?
¿Está hecho a mano?
¿ess-TA EH-cho ah MA-no?

... hand embroidered?
... bordado a mano?
*... bor-DA-doh ah
MA-no?*

May I try it on?
¿Puedo probármelo?
¿PWEH-doh pro-BAR-meh-lo?

That suits you marvelously.
Le queda muy bien.
leh KEH-da mwee b'yen.

Can you alter it?
¿Puede arreglarlo?
¿PWEH-deh ah-rreh-GLAR-lo?

Good. I'll take it.
Bien. Lo tomo.
b'yen. lo TOH-mo.

Will you wrap it?
¿Quiere envolverlo?
¿K'YEH-reh en-vohl-VEHR-lo?

Can you send it to this address?
¿Puede mandarlo a esta dirección?
¿PWEH-deh mahn-DAR-lo ah ESS-ta dee-rek-S'YOHN?

Can one pay by check?
¿Se puede pagar con cheque?
¿seh PWEH-deh pa-GAR kohn CHEH-keh?

A receipt, please.
Un recibo, por favor.
oon reh-SEE-bo, por fa-VOR.

The change, please.
El cambio, por favor.
el KAHM-b'yo, por fa-VOR.

Come see us again!
¡Venga a vernos de nuevo!
¡VEN-ga ah VEHR-nohs deh NWEH-vo!

Sale
Venta
VEN-ta

Bargains
Gangas
GAHN-gahs

Point to the Answer

Sírvase indicar en esta página su contestación a mi pregunta. Muchas gracias.
Please point on this page to your answer to my question. Thank you very much.

No tenemos.
We haven't any.

Es todo lo que tenemos de esta clase.
That's all we have of this type.

No tenemos más grande.
We haven't any larger.

No tenemos más chico.
We haven't any smaller.

No tenemos servicio de entrega.
We don't have delivery service.

Podemos mandarlo a una dirección en los Estados Unidos.
We can send it to an address in the United States.

¿Cuál es su dirección?
What is your address?

No aceptamos cheques personales.
We don't accept personal checks.

Aceptamos cheques viajeros.
We accept travelers checks.

Clothes

a blouse
una blusa
OO-na BLOO-sa

a skirt
una falda
OO-na FAHL-da

a (woman's) suit
un taller
oon tahl-YEHR.

a coat
un abrigo
oon ah-BREE-go

a hat
un sombrero
oon sohm-BREH-ro

a scarf
una bufanda
OO-na boo-FAHN-da

a handbag
una cartera
OO-na kar-TEH-ra

gloves
guantes
GWAHN-tehs

a dress (or) suit
un vestido
oon vess-TEE-doh

handkerchiefs
pañuelos
pahn-YWEH-lohs

a shirt
una camisa
OO-na ka-MEE-sa

pants
pantalones
pahn-ta-LO-nehs

a (man's) suit
un traje
oon TRA-heh

a jacket
una chaqueta
OO-na cha-KEH-ta

socks
calcetines
kahl-seh-TEE-nehs

a tie
una corbata
OO-na kor-BA-ta

an undershirt
una camiseta
OO-na ka-mee-SEH-ta

undershorts
calzoncillos
kahl-sohn-SEEL-yohs

stockings
medias
MEH-d'yahs

a slip
un refajo
oon reh-FA-ho

a brassiere
un sostén
oon sohs-TEN

panties
pantaletas
pahn-ta-LEH-tahs

pajamas
piyama
pee-YA-ma

a nightgown
una camisa de
dormir
*OO-na ka-MEE-sa
deh dor-MEER*

a bathrobe
una bata
OO-na BA-ta

a swimsuit
un traje de baño
oon TRA-heh deh BAHN-yo

a raincoat
un impermeable
oon eem-pehr-meh-AH-bleh

boots
botas
BO-tahs

sandals
sandalias
sahn-DA-l'yahs

shoes
zapatos
sa-PA-tohs

slippers
chinelas
chee-NEH-lahs

Sizes—Colors—Materials

.What size?
¿Qué tamaño?
¿Keh ta-MAHN-yo?

small
pequeño
peh-KEN-yo

medium
medio
MEH-d'yo

large
grande
GRAHN-deh

extra large
extra grande
EX-tra GRAHN-deh

larger
más grande
mahs GRAHN-deh

smaller
más pequeño
mahs peh-KEN-yo

wider
más ancho
mahs AHN-cho

narrower
más angosto
mahs ahn-GOHS-toh

longer
más largo
mahs LAR-go

shorter
más corto
mahs KOR-toh

What color?
¿De qué color?
¿deh keh ko-LOR?

red
rojo
RO-ho

blue
azul
ah-SOOL

yellow
amarillo
ah-ma-REEL-yo

orange
anaranjado
ah-na-rahn-HA-doh

green
verde
VEHR-deh

purple
violeta
v'yo-LEH-ta

brown
marrón
ma-RROHN

gray
gris
greess

tan
crema
KREH-ma

black
negro
NEH-gro

white
blanco
BLAHN-ko

darker
más oscuro
mahs ohs-KOO-ro

lighter
más claro
mahs KLA-ro

Is it silk?	linen	velvet	wool
¿Es de seda?	lino	terciopelo	lana
¿ess deh SEH-da?	*LEE-no*	*tehr-s'yo-PEH-lo*	*LA-na*

cotton	lace	nylon	dacron
algodón	encaje	nilón	dacrón
ahl-go-DOHN	*en-KA-heh*	*nee-LOHN*	*da-KROHN*

leather	suede
cuero	gamuza
KWEH-ro	*ga-MOO-sa*

kid	plastic	fur
cabretilla	plástico	piel
ka-breh-TEEL-ya	*PLAHS-tee-ko*	*p'yehl*

What kind of fur?	fox
¿Qué clase de piel?	zorro
¿keh KLA-seh deh p'yehl?	*SO-rro*

beaver	seal	mink	chinchilla
castor	foca	visón	chinchilla
kahs-TOR	*FO-ka*	*vee-SOHN*	*cheen-CHEEL-ya*

Newsstand

I would like . . .	. . . a guidebook.
Me gustaría . . .	. . . una guía.
meh goo-sta-REE-ya . . .	*OO-na GHEE-ya.*

. . . a map of the city.
. . . un mapa de la ciudad.
. . . oon MA-pa deh la s'yoo-DAHD.

... **postcards.**
... tarjetas postales.
... *tar-HEH-tahs pos-TA-lehs*

... **this paper.**
... este periódico.
... *ESS-teh peh-R'YO- dee-ko.*

... **that magazine.**
... esa revista.
... *ES-sa reh-VEESS-ta.*

... **A newspaper in English.**
... un periódico en inglés.
... *oon pehr-YO-dee-ko en een-GLEHS.*

Tobacco Shop

Have you American cigarettes?
¿Tiene cigarrillos americanos?
¿T'YEH-neh see-gar-REEL-yohs ah-meh-ree-KA-nohs?

cigars	**a pipe**	**tobacco**
tabacos	una pipa	picadura
ta-BA-kohs	*OO-na PEE-pa*	*pee-ka-DOO-ra*

matches	**a lighter**	**lighter fluid**
fósforos	encendedor	bencina
FOHS-fo-rohs	*en-sen-deh-DOHR*	*ben-SEE-na*

Drugstore

a toothbrush	**toothpaste**
un cepillo de dientes	pasta de dientes
oon seh-PEEL-yo deh D'YEN-tehs	*PAHS-ta deh D'YEN-tehs*

a safety razor
una navaja de seguridad
*OO-na na-VA-ha deh
seh-goo-ree-DAHD*

razor blades
hojillas
oh-HEEL-yahs

shaving cream
crema de afeitar
KREH-ma deh ah-fay-TAR

cologne
colonia
ko-LO-n'ya

an electric razor
una máquina de afeitar
OO-na MA-kee-na deh ah-fay-TAR

a hairbrush
un cepillo
oon-seh-PEEL-yo

a comb
un peine
oon PAY-neh

aspirin
aspirina
ahs-pee-REE-na

iodine
yodo
YO-doh

scissors
tijeras
tee-HEH-rahs

a nail file
una lima de uñas
OO-na LEE-ma deh OON-yahs

antiseptic
antiséptico
ahn-tee-SEP-tee-ko

adhesive tape
esparadrapo
ess-pa-ra-DRA-po

coughdrops
pastillas para la tos
pahs-TEEL-yahs PA-ra la tohs

sunglasses
lentes de sol
LEN-tehs deh sohl

Cosmetics

make-up base
base
BAH-seh

powder
polvo
POHL-vo

lipstick
pintura de labio
peen-TOO-ra deh LA-b'yo

eye shadow
sombra
SOHM-bra

nail polish
pintura de uñas
peen-TOO-ra deh OON-yahs

eyebrow pencil
lápiz para las cejas
*LA-pees PA-ra lahs
  SEH-hahs*

cleansing cream
crema limpiadora
*KREH-ma leem-p'ya-
  DOH-ra*

cotton
algodón
ahl-go-DOHN

bobby pins
ganchitos
gahn-CHEE-tohs

hair spray
laca
LA-ka

shampoo
shampú
shahm-POO

perfume
perfume
pehr-FOO-meh

That smells good, doesn't it?
Eso huele bien, ¿verdad?
EH-so WEH-leh b'yen, ¿vehr-DAHD?

Hairdresser

shampoo and set
lavar y peinar
la-VAR ee pay-NAHR

the part
la raya
la RA-ya

like this
así
ah-SEE

a manicure
una manicura
OO-na ma-nee-KOO-rah

a tint
un tinte
oon TEEN-teh

lighter
más claro
mahs KLA-ro

darker
más oscuro
mahs ohs-KOO-ro

Barber

a shave	a haircut	a massage
afeitar	un corte de pelo	un masaje
ah-fay-TAR	*oon KOR-teh deh PEH-lo*	*oon ma-SA-heh*

Use scissors.	shorter	not too short
Use tijeras.	más corto	no demasiado corto
OO-seh tee-HEH-rahs.	*mahs KOR-toh*	*no deh-mahs-YA-doh KOR-toh*

on top	in back	the sides	That's fine.
arriba	atrás	los lados	Está bien.
ah-REE-ba	*ah-TRAHS*	*lohs LA-dohs*	*ess-TA b'yen.*

Food Market

I would like . . .	a dozen
Me gustaría . . .	una docena
meh goo-sta-REE-ya . . .	*OO-na doh-SEH-na*

of this	of that
de esto	de eso
deh ESS-toh	*deh ES-so.*

I want five.	Is this fresh?	What is this?
Quiero cinco.	¿Está fresco esto?	¿Qué es esto?
K'YEH-ro SEEN-ko.	*¿ess-TA FRES-ko ESS-toh?*	*¿keh ess ESS-toh?*

Three cans of this.	How much per kilo?
Tres latas de esto.	¿Cuánto cuesta el kilo?
tres LA-tahs deh ESS-toh.	*¿KWAHN-toh KWESS-ta el KEE-lo?*

Can one buy wine here?
¿Se puede comprar vino aquí?
¿seh PWEH-deh kohm-PRAR VEE-no ah-KEE?

Sherry.
Vino de Jerez.
VEE-no deh heh-REHS.

Put it in a bag, please.
Póngalo en una bolsa, por favor.
POHN-ga-lo en OO-na BOHL-sa, por fa-VOR.

A propósito: Weight is measured by the kilo (kilogram—kilogramo) rather than by the pound. One kilo is equivalent to 2.2 pounds.

Jewelry

I would like . . .
Quisiera . . .
kee-S'YEH-ra . . .

. . . a watch.
. . . un reloj.
. . . oon reh-LO

. . . a ring.
. . . un anillo.
. . . oon ah-NEEL-yo.

. . . a necklace.
. . . un collar.
. . . oon kohl-YAR.

. . . a bracelet
. . . un brazalete.
. . . oon bra-sa-LEH-teh.

. . . earrings.
. . . unos pendientes.
. . . OO-nos pen-D'YEN-tehs.

Is this gold?
¿Es esto oro?
¿ess ESS-toh OH-ro?

. . . platinum?
. . . platino?
. . . pla-TEE-no?

. . . silver?
. . . plata?
. . . PLA-ta?

Is it solid or gold-plated?
¿Es macizo o dorado?
¿ess ma-SEE-so oh do-RA-doh?

a diamond
un brillante
oon breel-YAHN-teh

pearls	**a ruby**	**a sapphire**
perlas	un rubí	un zafiro
PEHR-lahs	*oon roo-BEE*	*oon sa-FEE-ro*

an amethyst	**a topaz**	**an aquamarine**
una amatista	un topacio	una aguamarina
OO-na ah-ma-	*oon toh-PA-s'yo*	*OO-na ah-gwa-*
TEESS-ta		*ma-REE-na*

Antiques

What period is this?
¿De qué período es esto?
¿deh keh peh-REE-oh-doh
  ess ESS-toh?

It's beautiful.
Es bello.
ess BEL-yo.

But very expensive.
Pero muy caro.
PEH-ro mwee KA-ro.

How much is . . .
¿Cuánto cuesta . . .
¿KWAHN-toh
  KWESS-ta . . .

. . . this book?
. . . este libro?
. . . ESS-teh LEE-bro?

. . . this picture
. . . este cuadro?
. . . ESS-teh KWA-dro?

. . . this map?
. . . este mapa?
. . . ESS-teh MA-pa?

. . . this frame?
. . . este marco?
. . . ESS-teh MAR-ko?

. . . this piece of furniture?
. . . este mueble?
. . . ESS-teh MWEH-bleh?

Is it an antique?
¿Es una antigüedad?
¿ess OO-na ahn-tee-
  gweh-DAHD?

Can you ship it?
¿Puede mandarlo?
¿PWEH-deh mahn-
  DAR-lo?

To this address.
A esta dirección.
ah ESS-ta dee-rek-S'YOHN.

🔔 17. Telephone

Talking on the telephone is an excellent test of your ability to communicate in Spanish because you can't see the person you are talking to or use gestures to help get across your meaning. When asking for someone, simply say his name and add **por favor**. If you say the number instead of dialing it, say the numbers in pairs. 606642 would be 60-66-42: **sesenta—sesenta y seis—cuarenta y dos.**

Where is the telephone?
¿Dónde está el teléfono?
*¿DOHN-deh ess-TA el
teh-LEH-fo-no?*

The telephone operator.
La telefonista.
la teh-leh-fo-NEES-ta.

Hello!
¡Hola! *or* A ver. *or* ¡Dígame! *or* Bueno.
¡OH-la!   ah vehr.   ¡DEE-ga-meh!   BWEH-no.

Information.
Información.
een-for-ma-S'YOHN.

Long distance.
Larga distancia.
LAR-ga deess-TAHN-s'ya.

Please, the telephone number of ———.
Por favor, el número de teléfono de ———.
*por fa-VOR, el NOO-meh-ro deh teh-LEH-fo-no
deh ———.*

That was a wrong number.
Fue un número equivocado.
fweh oon NOO-meh-ro eh-kee-vo-KA-doh.

Get me, please, number ———.
Comuníqueme, por favor, con el número ———.
*ko-moo-NEE-keh-meh, por fa-VOR, kohn el
NOO-meh-ro ———.*

I want to call Los Angeles in the United States.
Quiero llamar Los Ángeles en los Estados Unidos.
*KYEH-ro l'ya-MAR lohs AHN-heh-lehs en lohs
ess-TA-dohs oo-NEE-dohs.*

**The number I am calling
is ———,**
Estoy llamando el
número ———,
*ess-TOY l'ya-MAHN-doh
el NOO-meh-ro ———,*

extension . . .
extensión . . .
ex-ten-S'YOHN . . .

Must I wait long?
¿Debo esperar mucho tiempo?
¿DEH-bo ess-peh-RAR MOO-cho TYEM-po?

How much is it per minute?
¿Cuánto cuesta por minuto?
¿KWAHN-toh KWESS-ta por mee-NOO-toh?

My number is 31–01–38.
Mi número es treinta y uno–cero uno–treinta y ocho.
*mee NOO-meh-ro ess TRAIN-ta ee OO-no SEH-ro
OO-no TRAIN-ta ee OH-cho.*

Mr. Duran, please.
El señor Durán, por favor.
el sen-YOR doo-RAHN, por fa-VOR.

What?
¿Cómo?
¿KO-mo?

He (she) isn't here.
No está aquí.
no ess-TA ah-KEE.

Hold the line!
¡No cuelgue!
¡no KWEL-geh!

**When is he (she) coming
back?**
¿Cuándo vuelve?
¿KWAHN-do VWEL-veh?

Very well, I'll call back.
Bien, llamaré otra vez.
b'yen, l'ya-ma-REH OH-tra vess.

Can you take a message?
¿Puede tomar un recado?
¿PWEH-deh toh-MAR oon reh-KA-doh?

Ask him (her) to call me.
Dígale que me llame.
DEE-ga-leh keh meh L'YA-meh.

I'll give you my number.
Le daré mi número.
leh da-REH mee NOO-meh-ro.

Who is speaking?
¿Quién habla?
¿k'yen AH-bla?

This is Mr. Smith speaking.
Habla el señor Smith.
AH-bla el sen-YOR smith.

That is written: S–m–i–t–h.
Eso se escribe: S–m–i–t–h.
*EH-so seh es-KREE-beh: EH-seh EH-meh ee teh
AH-cheh.*

A	**B**	**C**	**CH**	**D**
ah	*beh*	*seh*	*cheh*	*deh*

E	**F**	**G**	**H**	**I**
eh	*EH-feh*	*heh*	*AH-cheh*	*ee*

J	**K**	**L**	**LL**	**M**
HO-ta	*ka*	*EH-leh*	*EHL-yeh*	*EH-meh*

N	Ñ	O	P	Q
EH-neh	*EHN-yeh*	*oh*	*peh*	*koo*

R	RR	S	T	U
EH-reh	*EH-rreh*	*EH-seh*	*teh*	*oo*

V	W	X
veh	*DOH-bleh veh*	*EH-kees*

Y	Z
ee-gree-YEH-ga	*SEH-ta*

A propósito: As American and English names are often strange to Spanish ears, you will find the spelled out alphabet very useful for spelling your name when you leave a message.

Where is the public telephone?
¿Dónde está el teléfono público?
¿DOHN-deh ess-TA el teh-LEH-fo-no POO-blee-ko?

The telephone book.
La guía telefónica.
la GHEE-ya teh-leh-FO-nee-ka.

Excuse me.	**What coin do I put in?**
Perdón.	¿Qué moneda debo echar?
pehr-DOHN.	*¿keh mo-NEH-da DEH-bo eh-CHAR?*

In Spain, tokens are used in public telephones.

A token, please.	**Another token.**
Una ficha, por favor.	Otra ficha.
·*OO-na FEE-cha, por fa-VOR.*	*OH-tra FEE-cha.*

If there is no public telephone available:

May I use your phone? **Certainly.**
¿Me permite usar su   Cómo no.
teléfono?   *KO-mo no.*
¿meh pehr-MEE-teh oo-
SAR soo teh-LEH-fo-no?

How much do I owe you? **Nothing.**
¿Cuánto le debo?   Nada.
¿KWAHN-toh leh DEH-bo? *NA-da.*

18. Post Office and Telegrams

One of the first things one does when abroad is to write postcards—tarjetas postales—to friends and relatives. Here is how to mail them. You might also impress your friends by adding a few words in Spanish, which you find at the end of this section.

Where is the post office?
¿Dónde está el correo?
¿DOHN-deh ess-TA el ko-RREH-oh?

Ten 50-centavo stamps.
Diez estampillas de a cincuenta.
dyess ess-tahm-PEEL-yahs deh ah seen-KWEHN-ta.

How much is needed?   **Air mail.**
¿Cuánto se necesita?   Por avión.
¿KWAHN-toh seh neh-seh-   *por ahv-YOHN.*
SEE-ta?

For a letter to the United States.
Para una carta a los Estados Unidos.
PA-ra OO-na KAR-ta ah los ess-TA-dohs oo-NEE-dohs.

... to Canada.   **... to England.**   **... to Australia.**
... al Canadá   ... a Inglaterra.   ... a Australia.
... ahl ka-na-   *... ah een-gla-*   *... ah ow-*
DA.   *TEH-ra.*   *STRAHL-ya.*

For names of other important countries, see dictionary.

Registered.   **Insured.**
Certificada.   Asegurada.
sehr-tee-fee-KA-da.   *ah-seh-goo-RA-da.*

Where can I send a telegram?
¿Dónde puedo mandar un telegrama?
¿DOHN-deh PWEH-doh mahn-DAR oon teh-leh-GRA-ma?

How much is it per word?
¿Cuánto cuesta por palabra?
¿KWAHN-toh KWESS-ta por pa-LA-bra?

I need writing paper.
Necesito papel de escribir.
neh-seh-SEE-toh pa-PEL deh es-kree-BEER.

. . . envelopes.
. . . sobres.
. . . SO-brehs.

Can you lend me
¿Puede prestarme
¿PWEH-deh press-TAR-meh

. . . a pen?
. . . una pluma?
. . . OO-na PLOO-ma?

. . . a pencil?
. . . un lápiz?
. . . oon LA-peess?

. . . some stamps?
. . . algunas estampillas?
. . . ahl-GOO-nahs ess-tahm-PEEL-yahs?

Dear John,
Querido Juan,
keh-REE-doh hwan,

Dear Jane,
Querida Juanita,
keh-REE-da hwa-NEE-ta,

Best regards from Acapulco.
Recuerdos desde Acapulco.
reh-KWEHR-dohs DES-deh ah-ka-POOL-ko.

Best wishes to everyone.
Saludos a todos.
sal-LOO-dohs ah TOH-dohs.

I miss you.
Te estraño mucho.
teh ess-TRA-n'yo MOO-cho.

With fond regards,
Cariñosamente,
ka-reen-yo-sa-MEN-teh,

19. Seasons and the Weather

---

winter
el invierno
el een-V'YEHR-no

spring
la primavera
la pree-ma-VEH-ra

summer
el verano
el veh-RA-no

autumn
el otoño
el oh-TOHN-yo

How is the weather?
¿Qué tiempo hace?
¿keh T'YEM-po AH-seh?

The weather is fine.
Hace buen tiempo.
AH-seh bwehn T'YEM-po.

It's cold.
Hace frío.
AH-seh FREE-yo.

It's raining.
Está lloviendo.
ess-TA l'yo-V'YEN-doh.

It's very hot.
Hace mucho calor.
AH-seh MOO-cho ka-LOR.

Let's go swimming.
Vamos a nadar.
VA-mohs ah na-DAR.

Where is the pool?
¿Dónde está la piscina?
¿DOHN-deh ess-TA la pee-SEE-na?

I need an umbrella.
Necesito un paraguas.
neh-seh-SEE-toh oon pa-RA-gwahs.

. . . boots.
. . . botas.
. . . BO-tahs.

. . . a raincoat.
. . . un impermeable.
. . . oon eem-pehr-meh-AH-bleh.

What a fog!
¡Qué neblina!
¡keh neh-BLEE-na!

One can't see.
No se puede ver.
no seh PWEH-deh vehr.

It's snowing.
Está nevando.
ess-TA neh-
VAHN-doh.

Do you like to ski?
¿Le gusta esquiar?
¿leh GOOS-ta
ess-kee-YAR?

... to skate?
... patinar?
... pa-tee-
NAR?

I want to rent skis.
Quiero alquilar esquíes.
K'YEH-ro ahl-kee-LAR
ess-KEE-ess.

... skates
... patines.
... pa-TEE-nehs.

A propósito: Temperature is expressed in centigrade, not Fahrenheit. Zero is freezing in centigrade; boiling is 100.

20. Doctor and Dentist

Doctor

I feel ill.
Me siento enfermo.
*meh S'YEN-toh
en-FEHR-mo.*

I need a doctor.
Necesito un médico.
*neh-seh-SEE-toh oon
MEH-dee-ko.*

It's urgent.
Es urgente.
ess oor-HEN-teh.

When can he come?
¿Cuándo puede venir?
*¿KWAHN-do PWEH-deh
veh-NEER?*

**Well, what's wrong with
you?**
Bueno, ¿qué le pasa?
BWEH-no, ¿keh leh PA-sa?

I don't feel well.
No me siento bien.
no meh S'YEN-toh b'yen.

Where does it hurt?
¿Dónde le duele?
¿DOHN-deh leh DWEH-leh?

Here.
Aquí.
ah-KEE.

I have a pain . . .
Tengo dolor . . .
*TEN-go doh-
LOR . . .*

. . . in my head.
. . . de cabeza.
*. . . deh ka-BEH-
sa.*

**He (she) has a
pain . . .**
Tiene dolor . . .
*T'YEH-neh doh-
LOR . . .*

. . . in the throat.
. . . de garganta.
. . . deh gar-GAHN-ta.

. . . in the ear.
. . . de oído.
. . . deh oh-EE-doh.

. . . in the stomach.
. . . de estómago.
. . . deh ess-TOH-ma-go.

. . . in the back.
. . . de espalda.
. . . deh ess-PAHL-da.

I hurt my leg.
Me hice daño en la pierna.
meh EE-seh DAHN-yo en la P'YEHR-na.

... my ankle.
.... el tobillo.
... el toh-BEEL-yo.

... my foot.
... el pie.
... el p'yeh.

... my arm.
... el brazo.
... el BRA-so.

... my hand.
... la mano.
... la MA-no.

I am dizzy
Estoy mareado.
ess-TOY ma-reh-AH-doh.

I have a fever.
Tengo fiebre.
TEN-go F'YEH-breh.

I can't sleep.
No puedo dormir.
no PWEH-doh dor-MEER.

I have diarrhea.
Tengo diarrea.
TEN-go d'ya-RREH-ah.

A propósito: The centigrade scale is also used to measure body temperature. The normal body temperature is 36.7 degrees (98 degrees Fahrenheit). So if you have anything higher than that, you have a temperature—Ud. tiene calentura.

Since when?
¿Desde cuándo?
¿DES-deh KWAHN-doh?

Since yesterday.
Desde ayer.
Des-deh ah-YEHR.

Since two days ago.
Desde hace dos días.
DES-deh AH-seh dohs DEE-yahs.

What have you eaten?
¿Qué ha comido?
¿keh ah ko-MEE-doh?

Undress.
Desvístase.
des-VEESS-ta-seh.

Lie down.
Acúestese.
ah-KWESS-teñ-seh.

Stand up.
Levántase.
leh-VAHN-ta-seh.

Breathe deeply.
Respire hondo.
res-PEE-reh OHN-doh.

Open your mouth.
Abra la boca.
AH-bra la BO-ka.

Show me your tongue.
Enséñeme la lengua.
en-SEN-yeh-meh la LEN-gwah.

Cough.
Tosa.
TOH-sa.

Get dressed.
Vístase.
VEESS-ta-seh.

You must ...
Tiene que ...
T'YEH-neh keh ...

... stay in bed.
... quedarse en cama.
... keh-DAR-seh en KA-ma.

... go to the hospital.
... ir al hospital.
... eer ahl ohs-pee-TAHL.

Take this prescription.
Tome esta receta.
TOH-meh ESS-ta reh-SEH-ta.

Take these pills.
Tome estas pastillas.
TOH-meh ESS-tahs pahs-TEEL-yahs.

Is it serious?
¿Es serio?
¿ess SEH-r'yo?

It's not serious.
No es serio.
No ess SEH-r'yo.

Don't worry.
No se preocupe.
no seh preh-oh-KOO-peh.

You have ...
Tiene ...
T'YEH-neh ...

... indigestion.
... indigestión.
... een-dee-hehs-T'YOHN.

... an infection.
... una infeccíon.
... OO-na een-fek-S'YOHN.

... a cold.
... un resfriado.
... *oon res-free-AH-doh.*

... appendicitis.
... apendicitis.
... *ah-pen-dee-SEE-teess.*

... liver trouble.
... un problema del hígado.
... *oon pro-BLEH-ma del EE-ga-doh.*

... a heart attack.
... un ataque cardíaco.
... *oon ah-TA-keh car-DEE-ah-ko.*

Be careful.
Tenga cuidado.
TEN-ga kwee-DA-doh.

Don't eat too much.
No coma demasiado.
no KO-ma deh-ma-S'YA-doh.

Don't drink any alcohol.
No tome nada de alcohol.
no TOH-meh NA-da deh ahl-ko-OHL.

How do you feel today?
¿Qué tal se siente hoy?
¿keh tahl seh S'YEN-teh oy?

Badly.
Mal.
mahl.

Better.
Mejor.
meh-HOR.

Much better.
Mucho mejor.
MOO-cho meh-HOR.

Dentist

In the unlikely event that the dentist should hurt you, tell him ¡Pare! "Stop!" or ¡Espere un momento! "Wait a moment!" until you have time to regain your courage.

Can you recommend a dentist?
¿Puede recomendar un dentista?
¿PWEH-deh reh-ko-men-DAR oon den-TEES-ta?

I have a toothache.
Tengo un dolor de muela.
TEN-go oon doh-LOR deh MWEH-la.

It hurts here.
Me duele aquí.
meh DWEH-leh ah-KEE.

There is an infection.
Hay una infección.
I OO-na een-fek-S'YOHN.

You need a filling.
Necesita una calza.
neh-seh-SEE-ta OO-na KAHL-sa.

Will it take long?
¿Se demorará mucho?
¿seh deh-mo-ra-RA MOO-cho?

Just fix it temporarily.
Arréglela provisionalmente.
ah-RREH-gleh-la pro-vee-s'yo-nahl-MEN-teh.

This tooth must come out.
Tiene que sacarse esta muela.
T'YEH-neh keh sa-KAR-seh ESS-ta MWEH-la.

An injection for pain, please.
Una inyección para el dolor, por favor.
OO-na een-yek-S'YOHN PA-ra el doh-LOR, por ja-VOR.

Does it hurt?
¿Le duele?
¿leh DWEH-leh?

A little.
Un poco.
oon PO-ko.

Not at all.
En absoluto.
en ahb-so-LOO-toh.

Is that all?
¿Eso es todo?
¿EH-so ess TOH-doh?

What do I owe you?
¿Cuánto le debo?
¿KWAHN-toh leh DEH-bo?

21. Problems and Police

Although the situations suggested below may never happen to you, the words are useful to know, just in case!

Go away!
¡Váyase!
¡VA-ya-seh!

Leave me alone!
¡Déjeme tranquila!
¡DEH-heh-meh trahn-KEE-la!

Or I'll call a policeman.
O llamo a un policía.
oh L'YA-mo ah oon po-lee-SEE-ya.

Help!
¡Socorro!
¡so-KO-rro!

Police!
¡Policía!
¡po-lee-SEE-ya!

What's going on?
¿Qué es lo que pasa?
¿keh ess lo keh PA-sa?

This man is annoying me.
Este hombre me está molestando.
ESS-teh OHM-breh meh ess-TA mo-les-TAHN-doh.

Where is the police station?
¿Dónde está el cuartel de policía?
¿DOHN-deh ess-TA el kwahr-TEL deh po-lee-SEE-ya?

I have been robbed of . . .
Me han robado . . .
meh ahn ro-BA-doh . . .

. . . my wallet.
. . . la cartera.
. . . la kar-TEH-ra.

. . . my car.
. . . el auto.
. . . el OW-toh.

. . . my watch.
. . . el reloj.
. . . el reh-LO.

. . . jewelry.
. . . las prendas.
. . . lahs PREN-dahs.

... my suitcase.
... la maleta.
... *la ma-LEH-ta.*

... my passport.
... el pasaporte.
... *el pa-sa-POR-teh.*

Stop that man!
¡Paren a ese hombre!
¡PA-ren ah EH-seh OHM-breh!

Wait!
¡Espere!
¡ess-PEH-reh!

That's the one!
¡Ese es!
¡EH-seh ess.

He robbed me.
Me robó.
meh ro-BO.

Do you wish to make a complaint?
¿Quiere presentar una queja?
¿KYEH-reh preh-sen-TAR OO-na KEH-ha?

I am innocent.
Soy inocente.
soy ee-no-SEN-teh.

I haven't done anything.
No he hecho nada.
no eh EH-cho NA-da.

I don't recognize him.
No lo reconozco.
no lo reh-ko-NOHS-ko.

I need a lawyer.
Necesito un abogado.
neh-seh-SEE-toh oon ah-bo-GA-doh.

Notify the American Consul.
Notifique al cónsul americano.
no-tee-FEE-keh ahl KOHN-sool ah-meh-ree-KA-no.

It's nothing.
No es nada.
no ess NA-da.

It's a misunderstanding.
Es un malentendido.
ess oon mahl-en-ten-DEE-doh.

Don't worry.
No se preocupe.
no seh preh-oh-KOO-peh.

Can I go now?
¿Puedo irme ahora?
¿PWEH-doh EER-meh ah-OH-ra?

A propósito: Despite the subject matter at the beginning of this section, ladies should not be alarmed if appreciative comments are made to them by men who stroll by, *if* the commentators continue to stroll in the opposite direction. It is simply an old Spanish custom called **el piropo** and merely expresses one's admiration of the girl or woman one has just passed.

22. Housekeeping

The following chapter will be espe cially interesting for those who plan to stay longer in a Spanish country or have occasion to employ Spanish-speaking baby sitters or household help, abroad or even at home.

What is your name?
¿Cómo se llama Ud.?
¿KO-mo seh L'YA-ma oo-STED?

Where have you worked before?
¿Dónde ha trabajado antes?
¿DOHN-deh ah tra-ba-HA-doh AHN-tehs?

Do you know how to cook?
¿Sabe cocinar?
¿SA-beh ko-see-NAR?

Do you know how to take care of a baby?
¿Sabe cuidar un bebé?
¿SA-beh- kwee-DAR oon beh-BEH?

This is your room.
Ésta es su habitación.
ESS-ta ess soo ah-bee-ta-S'YOHN.

Thursday will be your day off.
El jueves será su día libre.
el HWEH-vehs seh-RA soo DEE-ya LEE-breh.

We will pay you ———— every week.
Le pagaremos ———— cada semana.
leh pa-ga-REH-mohs ———— KA-da seh-MA-na.

Please clean . . .
Por favor, limpie . . .
por fa-VOR,
  LEEM-p'yeh . . .

. . . the living room.
. . . la sala.
. . . la SA-la.

. . . the dining room.
. . . el comedor.
. . . el ko-meh-DOR.

. . . the bedroom.
. . . el dormitorio.
. . . el dor-mee-TOR-yo.

. . . the bathroom.
. . . el cuarto de baño.
. . . el KWAHR-toh deh
  BAHN-yo.

. . . the kitchen.
. . . la cocina.
. . . la ko-SEE-na.

Wash the dishes.
Lave los platos.
LA-veh los PLA-tohs.

Sweep the floor.
Barra el piso.
BA-rra el PEE-so.

Use the vacuum cleaner.
Use la aspiradora.
OO-seh la ahs-pee-ra-DOH-ra.

. . . the broom.
. . . la escoba.
. . . la ess-KO-ba.

Polish the silver.
Limpie los cubiertos de plata.
LEEM-p'yeh los koob-YEHR-tohs deh PLA-ta.

Make the beds.
Tienda las camas.
T'YEN-da las KA-mahs.

Change the sheets.
Cambie las sábanas.
KAHM-b'yeh las
  SA-ba-nahs.

Wash this.
Lave esto.
LA-veh ESS-toh.

Iron this.
Planche esto.
PLAHN-cheh ESS-toh.

Go to the market.
Vaya al mercado.
VA-ya ahl mehr-KA-doh.

Have you finished?
¿Ha terminado?
¿ah tehr-mee-NA-doh?

What do we need?   **Here is the list.**
¿Qué necesitamos?   Aquí está la lista.
¿keh neh-seh-see-TA-mohs?   *ah-KEE ess-TA la LEESTA.*

Put the meat in the refrigerator.
Ponga la carne en la nevera.
POHN-ga la KAR-neh en la neh-VEH-ra.

If someone calls, write the name here.
Si alguien llama, escriba el nombre aquí.
see AHL-g'yen L'YA-ma, ess-KREE-ba el NOHM-breh
   ah-KEE.

I'll be at this number.
Estaré en este número.
ess-ta-REH en ESS-teh NOO-meh-ro.

I'll be back at 4 o'clock.
Regresaré a las cuatro.
reh-greh-sa-REH ah las KWA-tro.

Feed the baby at ———.
Dele a comer al bebé a las ———.
DEH-leh ah ko-MEHR ahl beh-BEH ah lahs ———.

Bathe the child.
Bañe al niño.
BAHN-yeh ahl NEEN-yo.

Put him to bed at ———.
Acuéstelo a las ———.
ah-KWESS-teh-lo ah lahs ———.

Serve lunch at 2 o'clock.
Sirva el almuerzo a las dos.
SEER-va el ahl-MWEHR-so ah lahs dohs.

Did anyone call?
¿Ha llamado alguien?
¿ah l'ya-MA-doh AHL-g'yen?

We are having guests for dinner.
Tenemos invitados para la cena.
teh-NEH-mohs een-vee-TA-dohs PA-ra la SEH-na.

Serve dinner at 9 o'clock.
Sirva la cena a las nueve.
SEER-va la SEH-na ah lahs NWEH-veh.

⬛ 23. A New Type of Dictionary

The following dictionary supplies a list of English words and their translation into Spanish, which will enable you to make up your own sentences in addition to those given in the phrase book. By using these words, in conjunction with the following advice and short cuts, you will be able to make up hundreds of sentences by yourself. In general, only one Spanish equivalent is given for each English word—the one most useful to you—so you won't be in doubt about which word to use. Every word in this dictionary is followed by the phonetic pronunciation, so you will have no difficulty being understood.

All nouns are either masculine or feminine. If a noun ends in -o it is usually masculine; if it ends in -a it is usually feminine. Any *exceptions* are noted by "(m)" or "(f)" after the noun in the dictionary.

Adjectives usually follow the noun they go with. All adjectives in this dictionary are given in the masculine form only. If the adjective ends in -o, you must change the ending to -a when it goes with a feminine noun:

> the white hat   el sombrero blanco
> . (El is the masculine word for "the.")
> the white house   la casa blanca
> (La is the feminine word for "the.")

If the adjective does not end in -o, it is generally the same for both masculine and feminine.

Plurals are formed by adding -s to words ending in a vowel, or -es to words ending in a consonant. If a noun is plural, the article and adjectives that go with it must be in the plural form too:

> the white hats   los sombreros blancos
> (Los is the masculine plural word for "the.")

the white houses   **las casas blancas**
(**Las** is the feminine plural word for "the.")

The verbs in the dictionary are given in the infinitive form. In actual use, their endings change according to the subject. Although a full grammatical explanation is not within the scope of this book, the following explanations will help you to use and recognize the present tense of most of the verbs in the dictionary.

Verbs are divided into three groups, or "conjugations," according to their infinitive endings: -ar, -er, and -ir. **Hablar** (to speak), **aprender** (to learn), and **vivir** (to live) are examples of the first, second, and third conjugations. There are five important forms for each tense, depending on the "person" referred to. You can carry on a great deal of conversation using the present tense. Here is the present of **hablar**, which can serve as a model for all verbs of the first group:

(yo) **hablo**	I speak *or* I am speaking
(tú) **hablas**	you speak *or* you (familiar) are speaking
(él, ella, usted) **habla**	he, she speaks, you (sg) speak *or* he, she is speaking, you are speaking
(nosotros, nosotras) **hablamos**	we (m and f) speak *or* we are speaking
(ellos, ellas, ustedes) **hablan**	they (m and f), you (pl) speak *or* they, you are speaking

Following the same order, the present tense forms for **aprender** and **vivir**, our examples of the second and third verb conjugations, are:

   aprendo, aprendes, aprende, aprendemos, aprenden
   vivo, vives, vive, vivimos, viven

Did you notice that these last two groups are almost the same?

In conversation the words for "I," "you," he," "she," etc. are frequently dropped, because the ending of the verb shows the person referred to. We put these pronouns in parentheses to remind you of this. By listening to the endings -o, -s, -a or -e, mos, and -n, you can tell which person is doing the action. We have not indicated a pronoun for "it" as in Spanish everything is masculine or feminine and therefore "it" is "he" or "she." Usted (Ud.) and tú both mean "you." However, you should ordinarily use Ud., the polite form. Tú is the familiar form, used within the family, between close friends, among students, and to children.

Although the Spanish present tense of verbs is equivalent to both the English simple present tense and the present progressive tense, you can also use the Spanish present participle, with the present tense form of estar (to be), exactly like the English progressive. The present participle ends in -ando for the first conjugation and -iendo, for the second and third conjugations:

> I am eating. **Yo estoy comiendo.**

As some of the most important verbs are irregular, we have included such forms in sections of the phrase book at the time and place you will need to use them. To help you form your own sentences, the present tense of "to be," "to have," "to go," "to come," and "to want" is given in the dictionary as well.

As we have pointed out, you can do a lot of communicating by using simply the present tense. But, in addition, you can use the infinitive to express a variety of other concepts. To say something must be done or is necessary, use es necesario directly with the infinitive:

> I must leave. **Es necesario partir.**

To say you want to do something or to invite someone to do something, use querer (to want) with the infinitive of the second verb:

> I want to go. **Quiero ir.**
> Do you want to go? **¿Quiere ir?**

For the negative, use **no:**

> I don't want to go.   **No quiero ir.**

An easy way to express what will happen in the future is to use a present form of **ir** (to go)—**voy, vas, va, vamos, van**—with a (to) followed by the infinitive:

> I am going to speak.   **Voy a hablar.**

The easiest way to give commands or make requests is to put **sírvase** in front of the infinitive:

> Come in!   **¡Sírvase entrar!**
> Don't come in!   **¡Sírvase no entrar!**

To form the perfect tense (i.e., "I have spoken," etc.) use the present tense of the verb **haber,** which is **he, has, ha, hemos, han,** combined with the past participle of the verb you want to use. The **-ar** verbs change their ending to **-ado** for the past participle (**hablar—hablado**) while the **-er** and **-ir** verbs generally change to **-ido** (**aprender—aprendido**).

> I have spoken *or* I spoke   **He hablado**

For basic conversational purposes the perfect tense can double in use for the past tense.

When you see a verb with **-se** attached to the infinitive in the dictionary it means that it is reflexive and must use the reflexive pronouns **me, te, se,** and **nos** with the verb:

> to get up   **levantarse**
> I get up.   **(Yo) me levanto.**

Object pronouns are given within the dictionary. They come before the verb, except that when used with infinitives and imperatives they follow and are attached:

> I see her.   **(Yo) la veo.**
> I don't want to see her.   **No quiero verla.**

The possessive of nouns is expressed by **de:**

> Robert's house   **la casa de Roberto**

Possessive pronouns are listed in the dictionary. Observe that these pronouns agree in gender and number with the noun to which they refer (not with the gender of the person possessing as in English):

This hat is his (hers). **Este sombrero es el suyo.**
This house is his (hers). **Esta casa es la suya.**

With this advice and the indications given within the dictionary itself, you will be able to use this communicating dictionary for making up countless sentences on your own and to converse with anyone you may meet.

There is, of course, much more to Spanish than these few suggestions we have given you—including the subtleties and irregularities of the Spanish verbs, diminutives, augmentatives, the special use of pronouns, and the numerous idioms and sayings that reflect the wisdom, poetry, and history of Spanish culture. But you can effectively use this selected basic vocabulary as an important step, or even a springboard, to enter the wonderful world that is the Spanish heritage and, by practice, absorb and constantly improve your command of this beautiful language.

For, as the Spanish say, **El apetito viene comiendo**— "Appetite comes with eating." Once you see how easy this book makes communicating in Spanish and how rewarding it is to speak to people in their own language, you will have the impetus to progress on your own.

A

a, an	un (m), una (f)	*oon, OO-na*
(to be) able	poder	*po-DEHR*
about (concerning)	acerca de	*ah-SEHR-ka deh*
above	sobre	*SO-breh*
absent	ausente	*ow-SEN-teh*
accept	aceptar	*ah-sep-TAR*
accident	accidente (m)	*ahk-see-DEN-teh*
account	cuenta	*KWEN-ta*
across	a través de	*ah tra-VEHS deh*
act	acto	*AHK-toh*
actor	actor	*ahk-TOR*
actress	actriz	*ahk-TREESS*
address	dirección (f)	*dee-rek-S'YOHN*
admission	admisión (f)	*ahd-mee-S'YOHN*
advertisement	anuncio	*ah-NOON-s'yo*
advice	consejo	*kohn-SEH-ho*
(to be) afraid	tener miedo	*teh-NEHR M'YEH-doh*
Africa	África	*AH-free-ka*
after	después	*dess-PWEHSS*
afternoon	tarde (f)	*TAR-deh*
again	de nuevo	*deh NWEH-vo*
against	contra	*KOHN-tra*

age	edad (f)	*eh-DAHD*
agency	agencia	*ah-HEN-s'ya*
agent	agente (m)	*ah-HEN-teh*
ago	hace	*AH-seh*

(See page 33 for an example.)

(to) agree	concordar	*kohn-kor-DAR*
ahead	adelante	*ah-deh-LAHN-teh*
air	aire (m)	*I-reh*
air-conditioned	aire acondicionado	*I-reh ah-kohn-dee-s'yo-NA-doh*
.air mail	correo aéreo	*ko-RREH-oh ah-EH-reh-oh*
airplane	avión (m)	*ahv-YOHN*
airport	aeropuerto	*ah-eh-ro-PWER-toh*
all	todo	*TOH-doh*
That's all!	¡Eso es todo!	*¡ES-so ess TOH-doh!*
(to) allow	permitir	*pehr-mee-TEER*
all right	está bien	*ess-TA b'yen*
almost	casi	*KA-see*
alone	solo	*SO-lo*
already	ya	*ya*
also	también	*tahm-B'YEN*
always	siempre	*S'YEM-preh*
(I) am (permanent status)	soy	*soy*

(I) am (location or temporary status)	estoy	*ess-TOY*
America	América	*ah-MEH-ree-ka*
American	americano	*ah-meh-ree-KA-no*
amusing	divertido	*dee-ver-TEE-doh*
and	y	*ee*
angry	enojado	*eh-no-HA-doh*
animal	animal (m)	*ah-nee-MAHL*
ankle	tobillo	*toh-BEEL-yo*
annoying	molesto	*mo-LESS-toh*
another	otro	*OH-tro*
answer	respuesta	*ress-PWESS-ta*
antiseptic	antiséptico	*ahn-tee-SEP-tee-ko*
any	cualquier	*kwahl-K'YEHR*
anyone	alguien	*AHL-g'yen*
anyone (at all)	cualquiera	*kwahl-K'YEH-ra*
anything	algo	*AHL-go*
anywhere	en cualquier parte	*en kwahl-K'YEHR PAR-teh*
apartment	apartamento	*ah-par-ta-MEN-toh*
apple	manzana	*mahn-SA-na*
appointment	cita	*SEE-ta*
April	abril	*ah-BREEL*
Arab	árabe (m or f)	*AH-ra-beh*

Arabic (language)	árabe	*AH-ra-beh*
architecture	arquitectura	*ar-kee-tek-TOO-ra*
are (permanent status)		
(you sg.) are	(Ud.) es	*ess*
(we) are	(nosotros) somos	*SO-mohs*
(they, you pl.) are	(ellos, ellas, Uds.) son	*sohn*
are (location or temporary status)		
(you sg.) are	(Ud.) está	*ess-TA*
(we) are	(nosotros) estamos	*ess-TA-mohs*
(they, you pl.) are	(ellos, ellas, Uds.) están	*ess-TAHN*
(there) are	hay	*I*
Argentina	Argentina	*ar-hen-TEE-na*
Argentinian	Argentino	*ar-hen-TEE-no*
arm	brazo	*BRA-so*
army	ejército	*eh-HEHR-see-toh*
around (surrounding)	alrededor	*ahl-reh-deh-DOR*
around (approximately)	alrededor de	*ahl-reh-deh-DOR deh*
(to) arrive	llegar	*l'yeh-GAR*
art	arte (m)	*AR-teh*
artist (m or f)	artista	*ar-TEESS-ta*

as	como	*KO-mo*
Asia	Asia	*AH-s'ya*
(to) ask (a question).	preguntar	*preh-goon-TAR*
(to) ask for	pedir	*·peh-DEER*
asleep	dormido	*dor-MEE-doh*
asparagus	espárrago	*ess-PA-rra-go*
aspirin	aspirina	*ahs-pee-REE-na*
ass	asno	*AHS-no*
assortment	surtido	*soor-TEE-doh*
at (location)	en	*en*
at (time)	a	*ah*
Atlantic	Atlántico	*aht-LAHN-tee-ko*
atomic	atómico	*ah-TOH-mee-ko*
August	agosto	*ah-GOHS-toh*
aunt	tía	*TEE-ya*
Australia	Australia	*ows-TRA-l'ya*
Australian	australiano	*ows-tra-L'YA-no*
Austria	Austria	*OWS-tree-ya.*
author	autor (m)	*ow-TOR*
automatic	automático	*ow-toh-MA-tee-ko*
automobile	automóvil	*ow-toh-MO-veel*
autumn	otoño	*oh-TOHN-yo*
(to) avoid	evitar	*eh-vee-TAR*

B

baby	bebé (m)	*beh-BEH*
bachelor	soltero	*sohl-TEH-ro*
back (part of body)	espalda	*ess-PAHL-da*
bacon	tocino	*toh-SEE-no*
bad	malo	*MA-lo*
baggage	equipaje (m)	*eh-kee-PA-heh*
banana	banana	*ba-NA-na*
bandage	venda	*VEN-da*
bank	banco	*BAHN-ko*
bar	bar (m)	*bar*
barber	barbero	*bar-BEH-ro*
basement	sótano	*SO-ta-no*
bath	baño	*BAHN-yo*
bathing suit	traje de baño (m)	*TRA-heh deh BAHN-yo*
bathroom	cuarto de baño	*KWAHR-toh deh BAHN-yo*
battery	batería	*ba-teh-REE-ya*
battle	batalla	*ba-TAHL-ya*
(to) be (permanent status)	ser	*sehr*

(See also "am," "is," "are," "was," "were," "been.")

(to) be (location or temporary status)	estar	*ess-TAR*

(See also "am," "is," "are," "was," "were," "been.")

beach	playa	*PLA-ya*
beans	frijoles (m)	*free-HO-lehs*
bear	oso	*OH-so*
beard	barba	*BAR-ba*
beautiful	bello	*BEL-yo*
beauty	belleza	*bel-YEH-sa*
beauty shop	salón de belleza (m)	*sa-LOHN deh bel-YEH-sa*
because	porque	*por-KEH*
bed	cama	*KA-ma*
bedroom	alcoba	*ahl-KO-ba*
bedspread	cubrecama (m)	*koo-breh-KA-ma*
beef	carne de res (f)	*KAR-neh deh rehs*
been (permanent status)	sido	*SEE-doh*
been (location or temporary status)	estado	*ess-TA-doh*
beer	cerveza	*sehr-VEH-sa*
before	antes	*AHN-tehs*
(to) begin	empezar	*em-peh-SAR*
behind	detrás	*deh-TRAHS*
(to) believe	creer	*kreh-EHR*
below	debajo	*deh-BA-ho*
belt	cinturón (m)	*seen-too-ROHN*
beside	al lado	*ahl LA-doh*

besides	además	ah-deh-MAHS
best (adj.)	el (la) mejor	el (la) meh-HOR
best (adv.)	lo mejor	lo meh-HOR
better	mejor	meh-HOR
between	entre	EN-treh
bicycle	bicicleta	bee-see-KLEH-ta
big	grande	GRAHN-deh
bill	cuenta	KWEN-ta
bird	pájaro	PA-ha-ro
birthday	cumple-años (m)	'koom-pleh-AHN-yohs
black	negro	NEH-gro
blanket	frazada	fra-SA-da
blond	rubio	ROO-byo
blood	sangre (f)	SAHN-gr eh
blouse	blusa	BLOO-sa
blue	azul	ah-SOOL
boardinghouse	casa de huéspedes	KA-sa deh WEHS-peh-dehs
boat	barco	BAR-ko
body	cuerpo	KWEHR-po
Bolivia	Bolivia	bo-LEEV-ya
Bolivian	boliviano	bo-leev-YA-no
book	libro	LEE-bro
bookstore	librería	lee-breh-REE-ya
born	nacido	na-SEE-doh

(to) borrow	pedir prestado	*peh-DEER press-TA-doh*
boss	jefe	*HEH-feh*
both	ambos	*AHM-bohs*
(to) bother	molestar	*mo-less-TAR*
bottle	botella	*bo-TEL-ya*
bottom	fondo	*FOHN-doh*
bought	comprado	*kohm-PRA-doh*
boy	muchacho	*moo-CHA-cho*
brain	cerebro	*seh-REH-bro*
brake	freno	*FREH-no*
brave	valiente	*va-L'YEN-teh*
Brazil	Brasil	*bra-SEEL*
Brazilian	brasileño	*bra-see-LEN-yo*
bread	pan (m)	*pahn*
(to) break	romper	*rohm-PEHR*
breakfast	desayuno	*deh-sa-YOO-no*
(to) breathe	respirar	*res-pee-RAR*
bridge	puente (m)	*PWEN-teh*
briefcase	maletín (m)	*ma-leh-TEEN*
(to) bring	traer	*tra-EHR*
Bring me ...	Tráigame ...	*TRY-ga-meh ...*
broken	roto	*RO-toh*
brother	hermano	*ehr-MA-no*
brother-in-law	cuñado	*koon-YA-doh*

brown	pardo, marrón	*PAR-doh, ma-ROHN*
brunette	morena	*mo-REH-na*
(to) build	construir	*kohn-stroo-EER*
building	edificio	*eh-dee-FEE-s'yo*
built	construído	*kohn-stroo-EE-doh*
bull	toro	*TOH-ro*
bullfight	corrida de toros	*ko-RREE-da deh TOH-rohs*
bullfighter	torero	*toh-REH-ro*
bullring	plaza de toros	*PLA-sa deh TOH-rohs*
bureau	cómoda	*KO-mo-da*
bus	autobús (m)	*ow-toh-BOOSS*
bus stop	parada de autobús	*pa-RA-da deh ow-toh-BOOSS*
business	negocio	*neh-GO-s'yo*
busy	ocupado	*oh-koo-PA-doh*
but	pero	*PEH-ro*
butter	mantequilla	*mahn-teh-KEEL-ya*
button	botón (m)	*bo-TOHN*
(to) buy	comprar	*kohm-PRAR*
by	por	*por*

C

cab	taxi (m)	*TAHX-see*
cabbage	repollo	*reh-POL-yo*
cable	cable (m)	*KA-bleh*

cake	torta	TOR-ta
(to) call	llamar	l'ya-MAR
Call me.	Llámeme.	L'YA-meh-meh.
camera	cámara	KA-ma-ra
can (to be able)	poder	po-DEHR
Can you ... ?	¿Puede Ud. ... ?	¿PWEH-deh oo-STED ... ?
(I) can	puedo	PWEH-doh
(I) can't	no puedo	no PWEH-doh
can (container)	lata	LA-ta
can opener	abrelatas	ah-breh-LA-tahs
candy	dulce (m)	DOOL-seh
cap	gorra	GO-rra
capable	capaz	ka-PAHS
cape	capa	KA-pa
captain	capitán (m)	ka-pee-TAHN
car	automóvil (m)	ow-toh-MO-veel
carburetor	carburador (m)	kar-boo-ra-DOR
card	tarjeta	tar-HEH-ta
(to take) care of	cuidar	kwee-DAR
(Be) careful!	¡Tenga cuidado!	¡TEN-ga kwee-DA-doh!
careless	descuidado	des-kwee-DA-doh
Caribbean	Caribe	ka-REE-beh
carrot	zanahoria	sa-na-OHR-ya
(to) carry	llevar	l'yeh-VAR

Carry this to . . .	Lleve esto a . . .	L'YEH-veh ESS-toh ah . . .
cashier	cajero	ka-HEH-ro
castle	castillo	kahs-TEEL-yo
cat	gato	GA-toh
cathedral	catedral (f)	ka-teh-DRAHL
catholic	católico	ka-TOH-lee-ko
celebration	celebración (f)	seh-leh-bra-S'YOHN
cemetery	cementerio	seh-men-TEH-r'yo
cent	centavo	sen-TA-vo
center	centro	SEN-tro
century	siglo	SEE-glo
certainly	seguramente	seh-goo-ra-MEN-teh
certificate	certificado	serh-tee-fee-KA-doh
chair	silla	SEEL-ya
chandelier	araña	ah-RAHN-ya
change	cambio	KAHM-b'yo
(to) change	cambiar	kahm-B'YAR
charming	encantador	en-kahn-ta-DOR
chauffeur	chofer	cho-FEHR
cheap	barato	ba-RA-toh
check	cheque (m)	CHEH-keh
checkroom	guarda-ropa (m)	gwahr-da-RRO-pa
cheese	queso	KEH-so
chest	pecho	PEH-cho

chicken	pollo	POHL-yo
child	niño (m), niña (f)	NEEN-yo, NEEN-ya
Chile	Chile	CHEE-leh
Chilean	chileno	chee-LEH-no
China	China	CHEE-na
Chinese	chino	CHEE-no
chocolate	chocolate (m)	cho-ko-LA-teh
chop	chuleta	choo-LEH-ta
church	iglesia	ee-GLEH-s'ya
cigar	cigarro	see-GA-rro
cigarette	cigarrillo	see-ga-REEL-yo
city	ciudad (f)	s'yoo-DAHD
(to) clean	limpiar	leem-P'YAR
clear	claro	KLA-ro
clever	hábil	AH-beel
climate	clima (m)	KLEE-ma
close	cerca	SEHR-ka
(to) close	cerrar	seh-RRAR
closed	cerrado	seh-RRA-doh
clothes	ropa	RO-pa
coast	costa	KO-sta
coat	abrigo	ah-BREE-go
coffee	café (m)	ka-FEH
coin	moneda	mo-NEH-da

cold	frío	*FREE-yo*
college	universidad (f)	*oo-nee-vehr-see-DAHD*
Colombia	Colombia	*ko-LOHM-b'ya*
Colombian	colombiano	*ko-lohm-B'YA-no*
colonel	coronel (m)	*ko-ro-NEL*
color	color (m)	*ko-LOR*
(to) come	venir	*veh-NEER*
(I) come (am coming)	vengo	*VEN-go*
(you sg.) come (are coming)	(Ud.) viene	*V'YEH-neh*
(he, she) comes (is coming)	(él, ella) viene	*V'YEH-neh*
(we) come (are coming)	(nosotros) venimos	*veh-NEE-mohs*
(they, you pl.) come (are coming)	(ellos, ellas, Uds.) vienen	*V'YEH-nen*
Come!	¡Venga!	*¡VEN-ga!*
Come in!	¡Adelante!	*¡Ah-deh-LAHN-teh!*
(to) come back	volver	*vohl-VEHR*
comb	peine (m)	*PAY-neh*
company	compañía	*kohm-pahn-YEE-ya*
competition	competencia	*kohm-peh-TEN-s'ya*
complete	completo	*kohm-PLEH-toh*

computer	máquina calculadora	*MA-kee-na kahl-koo-la-DOH-ra*
concert	concierto	*kohn-S'YEHR-toh*
congratulations	felicitaciones (f)	*feh-lee-see-ta-S'YO-nehs*
conservative	conservador	*kohn-sehr-va-DOR*
(to) continue	continuar	*kohn-teen-WAHR*
conversation	conversación (f)	*kohn-vehr-sa-S'YOHN*
cook	cocinero	*ko-see-NEH-ro*
(to) cook	cocinar	*ko-see-NAR*
cool	fresco	*FRÉSS-ko*
copy	copia	*KO-p'ya*
corkscrew	sacacorchos (m)	*sa-ka-KOR-chohs*
corn	maíz (m)	*ma-EESS*
corner (street)	esquina	*ess-KEE-na*
corner (room)	rincón (m)	*reen-KOHN*
correct	correcto	*ko-RREK-toh*
(to) cost	costar	*kohs-TAR*
Costa Rica	Costa Rica	*KOHS-ta REE-ka*
Costa Rican	costarricense	*kohs-ta-rree-SEN-seh*
cotton	algodón (m)	*ahl-go-DOHN*
cough	tos (f)	*tohs*
could	poder	*po-DEHR*

Use the appropriate form of *poder* listed here, with the infinitive of the principal verb

(I, you sg., he, she) could	(yo, Ud., él ella) podría	*po-DREE-ah*
(we) could	podríamos	*po-DREE-ah-mohs*
(they, you pl.) could	podrían	*po-DREE-ahn*
country	país (m)	*pah-EESS*
cousin	primo	*PREE-mo*
cow	vaca	*VA-ka*
crab	cangrejo	*kahn-GREH-ho*
(to) crate	embalar	*em-ba-LAR*
crazy	loco	*LO-ko*
cream	crema	*KREH-ma*
(to) cross	cruzar	*kroo-SAR*
crossing	cruce (m)	*KROO-seh*
cup	taza	*TA-sa*
custom (habit)	costumbre (f)	*kohs-TOOM-breh*
customs (office)	aduana	*ah-DWA-na*
customs form	formulario de de aduana	*for-moo-LA-r'yo deh ah-DWA-na*
(to) cut	cortar	*kor-TAR*

D

(to) dance	bailar	*by-LAR*
dangerous	peligroso	*peh-lee-GRO-so*

dark	oscuro	*ohs-KOO-ro*
darling	querido	*keh-REE-doh*
date (calendar)	fecha	*FEH-cha*
date (appoint- ment)	cita	*SEE-ta*
daughter	hija	*EE-ha*
daughter-in-law	nuera	*NWEH-ra*
day	día (m)	*DEE-ya*
dead	muerto	*MWEHR-toh*
dear	querido	*keh-REE-doh*
December	diciembre	*dee-S'YEM-breh*
(to) decide	decidir	*deh-see-DEER*
deck (boat)	cubierta	*koo-B'YEHR-ta*
deep	hondo	*OHN-doh*
delay	demora	*deh-MO-ra*
delicious	delicioso	*deh-lee-S'YO-so*
delighted	encantado	*en-kahn-TA-doh*
dentist	dentista (m)	*den-TEESS-ta*
department store	tienda de de- partamentos	*T'YEN-da deh deh- par-ta-MEN-tohs*
desert	desierto	*deh-S'YEHR-toh*
desk	escritorio	*es-kree-TOR-yo*
dessert	postre (m)	*POHS-treh*
detour	desvío	*des-VEE-yo*
devil	diablo	*D'YA-blo*
dictionary	diccionario	*deek-s'yo-NA-r'yo*

different	diferente	dee-feh-REN-teh
difficult	difícil	dee-FEE-seel
(to) dine	cenar	seh-NAR
dining room	comedor (m)	ko-meh-DOR
dinner	cena	SEH-na
direction	dirección (f)	dee-rek-S'YOHN
dirty	sucio	SOO-s'yo
disappointed	desilusionado	deh-see-loo-s'yo-NA-doh
discount	descuento	des-KWEN-toh
divorced	divorciado	dee-vor-S'YA-doh
dizzy	mareado	ma-reh-AH-doh
(to) do	hacer	ah-SEHR

Do not translate the word "do" when it is used to make a question or a negative sentence in English. To ask a question in Spanish, put the subject after the verb, or simply make the sentence a question by the tone of your voice. To make a negative sentence, simply use no before the verb.

Do you want . . . ?	¿Quiere Ud. . . ?	¿K'YEH-reh oo-STED . . . ?

(Don't . . . use sírvase no with the verb. See p. 140 for usage.)

Don't you want . . . ?	¿No quiere . . . ?	¿no K'YEH-reh . . . ?
Don't do that!	¡No haga eso!	¡no AH-ga EH-so!
dock	muelle (m)	MWEL-yeh
doctor	médico	MEH-dee-ko

dog	perro	*PEH-rro*
dollar	dólar (m)	*DOH-lar*
door	puerta	*PWER-ta*
down	abajo	*ah-BA-ho*
downtown	el centro de la ciudad	*el SEN-tro deh la s'yoo-DAHD*
dress	vestido	*ves-TEE-doh*
(to) drink	beber	*beh-BEHR*
(to) drive	conducir	*kohn-doo-SEER*
driver	conductor	*kohn-dook-TOR*
driver's license	permiso de conducir	*pehr-MEE-so deh kohn-doo-SEER*
drugstore	farmacia	*far-MA-s'ya*
drunk	borracho	*bo-RRA-cho*
dry cleaner	tintorería	*teen-toh-reh-REE-ya*
duck	pato	*PA-toh*

E

each	cada	*KA-da*
ear (outer)	oreja	*oh-REH-ha*
ear (inner)	oído	*oh-EE-doh*
early	temprano	*tem-PRA-no*
(to) earn	ganar	*ga-NAR*
earth	tierra	*TYEH-rra*
east	este	*ESS-teh*
easy	fácil	*FA-seel*

(to) eat	comer	*ko-MEHR*
eggs	huevos	*WEH-vohs*
eight	ocho	*OH-cho*
eighteen	dieciocho	*d'yess-ee-OH-cho*
eight hundred	ochocientos	*oh-cho-S'YEN-tohs*
eighty	ochenta	*oh-CHEN-ta*
either, or	o	*oh*
either (one)	cualquiera	*kwahl-K'YEH-ra*
elbow	codo	*KO-doh*
electric	eléctrico	*eh-LEK-tree-ko*
elephant	elefante (m)	*eh-leh-FAHN-teh*
elevator	ascensor (m)	*ah-sen-SOR*
embarrassed	apenado	*ah-peh-NA-doh*
embassy	embajada	*em-ba-HA-da*
emergency	emergencia	*eh-mehr-HEN-s'ya*
employee	empleado	*em-pleh-AH-doh*
end	fin	*feen*
(to) end	terminar	*tehr-mee-NAR*
English	inglés (m),	*een-GLEHSS*
	inglesa (f)	*een-GLEH-sa*
entertaining	divertido	*dee-vehr-TEE-doh*
error	error	*eh-RROR*
especially	especialmente	*ess-peh-s'yahl-MEN-teh*
Europe	Europa	*eh-oo-RO-pa*
European	europeo	*eh-oo-ro-PEH-oh*

even	aun	*ah-OON*
evening	noche (f)	*NO-cheh*
ever (sometime)	alguna vez	*ahl-GOO-na vess*
every	cada	*KA-da*
everybody	todo el mundo	*TOH-doh el MOON-doh*
everything	todo	*TOH-doh*
exactly	exactamente	*ek-sahk-ta-MEN-teh*
excellent	excelente	*ek-seh-LEN-teh*
except	excepto	*ek-SEP-toh*
(to) exchange	cambiar	*kahm-B'YAR*
¡Excuse me!	¡Perdón!	*¡pehr-DOHN!*
exit	salida	*sa-LEE-da*
expensive	caro	*KA-ro*
experience	experiencia	*es-peh-R'YEN-s'ya*
explanation	explicación (f)	*es-plee-ka-S'YOHN*
(to) export	exportar	*es-por-TAR*
extra	extra	*ES-tra*
eye	ojo	*OH-ho*

F

face	cara	*KA-ra*
factory	fábrica	*FA-bree-ka*
fair (show)	feria	*FEH-r'ya*
fall	caída	*ka-EE-da*

fall (autumn)	otoño	*oh-TOHN-yo*
(to) fall	caer	*ka-EHR*
family	familia	*fa-MEEL-ya*
famous	famoso	*fa-MO-so*
far	lejos	*LEH-hohs*
How far?	¿A qué dis-tancia?	*¿ah keh dees-TAHN-s'ya?*
fare	pasaje (m)	*pa-SA-heh*
farm	hacienda	*ah-S'YEN-da*
farther	más lejos	*mahs LEH-hohs*
fast	rápido	*RA-pee-doh*
fat	gordo	*GOR-doh*
father	padre (m)	*PA-dreh*
father-in-law	suegro	*SWEH-gro*
February	febrero	*feh-BREH-ro*
(to) feel	sentir	*sen-TEER*
fever	fiebre (f)	*F'YEH-breh*
few	pocos	*PO-kohs*
fifteen	quince	*KEEN-seh*
fifty	cincuenta	*seen-KWEN-ta*
(to) fight	luchar	*loo-CHAR*
(to) fill	llenar	*l'yeh-NAR*
film	película	*peh-LEE-koo-la*
finally	finalmente	*fee-nahl-MEN-teh*
(to) find	encontrar	*en-kohn-TRAR*

(to) find out	descubrir	*des-koo-BREER*
finger	dedo	*DEH-doh*
(to) finish	terminar	*tehr-mee-NAR*
finished	terminado	*tehr-mee-NA-doh*
fire	fuego	*FWEH-go*
first	primero	*pree-MEH-ro*
fish (in the water)	pez	*pess*
fish (on the plate)	pescado	*pess-KA-doh*
(to) fish	pescar	*pess-KAR*
five	cinco	*SEEN-ko*
flight	vuelo	*VWEH-lo*
floor (of room)	suelo	*SWEH-lo*
floor (of a building)	piso	*PEE-so*
flower	flor (f)	*flor*
fly (insect)	mosca	*MOHS-ka*
(to) fly	volar	*vo-LAR*
food	comida	*ko-MEE-da*
foot	pie (m)	*p'yeh*
for (sake of time or value)	por	*por*
for (use, purpose or destination)	para	*PA-ra*
foreigner	extranjero	*es-trahn-HEH-ro*

forest	selva	*SEL-va*
(to) forget	olvidar	*ohl-vee-DAR*
Don't forget!	¡No se olvide!	*¡no seh ohl-VEE-deh!*
fork	tenedor (m)	*teh-neh-DOR*
forty	cuarenta	*kwa-REN-ta*
fountain	fuente (f)	*FWEN-teh*
four	cuatro	*KWA-tro*
fourteen	catorce	*ka-TOR-seh*
fox	zorro	*SO-rro*
France	Francia	*FRAHN-s'ya*
free	libre	*LEE-breh*
French	francés (m),	*frahn-SEHS*
	francesa (f)	*frahn-SEH-sa*
frequently	frecuentemente	*freh-kwen-teh-*
		MEN-teh
fresh	fresco	*FRES-ko*
Friday	viernes	*V'YEHR-ness*
fried	frito	*FREE-toh*
friend	amigo	*ah-MEE-go*
frog	rana	*RA-na*
from	desde	*DES-deh*
(in) front of	delante de	*deh-LAHN-teh deh*
fruit	fruta	*FROO-ta*
full	lleno	*L'YEH-no*
funny	gracioso	*gra-S'YO-so*
furniture	muebles (m)	*MWEH-blehs*

(in the) future	en el futuro	*en el foo-TOO-ro*
future tense	tiempo futuro	*TYEM-po foo-TOO-ro*

G

game	juego	*HWEH-go*
garage	garage (m)	*ga-RA-heh*
garden	jardín (m)	*har-DEEN*
gas	gas	*gahs*
gasoline	gasolina	*ga-so-LEE-na*
gas station	puesto de gasolina	*PWESS-toh deh ga-so-LEE-na*
general	general	*heh-neh-RAHL*
gentleman	caballero	*ka-bahl-YEH-ro*
German	alemán (m), alemana (f)	*ah-leh-MAHN ah-leh-MA-na*
Germany	Alemania	*ah-leh-MAHN-ya*
(to) get (to obtain)	conseguir	*kohn-seh-GHEER*
(to) get off	bajarse	*ba-HAR-seh*
(to) get on	subir :	*soo-BEER*
(to) to get out	salir	*sa-LEER*
Get out!	¡Fuera!	*¡FWEH-ra!*
(to) get up	levantarse	*leh-vahn-TAR-seh*
gift	regalo	*reh-GA-lo*
(to) give	dar	*dar*
Give me ...	Deme ...	*DEH-meh ...*

girl	muchacha	*moo-CHA-cha*
glass (for windows)	vidrio	*VEE-dree-yo*
glass (drinking)	vaso	*VA-so*
glasses	lentes (m)	*LEN-tehs*
glove	guante (m)	*GWAHN-teh*
(to) go	ir	*eer*
(I) go (am going)	voy	*voy*
(you sg.) go (are going)	(Ud.) va	*va*
(he, she) goes (is going)	(él, ella) va	*va*
(we) go (are going)	vamos	*VA-mohs*
(they, you pl.) go (are going)	(ellos, ellas, Uds.) van	*vahn*
Go away!	¡Váyase!	*¡VA-ya-seh!*
(to) go away	irse	*EER-seh*
(to) go back	regresar	*reh-greh-SAR*
(to) go on	continuar	*kohn-teen-WAHR*
Go on!	¡Continúe!	*¡kohn-tee-NOO-eh!*
goat	cabra	*KA-bra*
God	Dios (m)	*d'yohs*
gold	oro	*OH-ro*
golf	golf (m)	*gohlf*
good	bueno	*BWEH-no*

goodbye	adiós	*ah-D'YOHS*
government	gobierno	*go-B'YEHR-no*
grandfather	abuelo	*ah-BWEH-lo*
grandmother	abuela	*ah-BWEH-la*
grapes	uvas	*OO-vahs*
grateful	agradecido	*ah-gra-deh-SEE-doh*
gray	gris	*greess*
great (before a noun)	gran	*grahn*
great (after a noun or alone)	grande	*GRAHN-deh*
a great many	muchos	*·MOO-chohs*
Greece	Grecia	*GREH-s'ya*
Greek	griego	*GR'YEH-go*
green	verde	*VEHR-deh*
group	grupo	*GROO-po*
Guatemala	Guatemala	*gwa-teh-MA-la*
Guatemalan	Guatemalteco	*gwa-teh-mahl-TEH-ko*
guide	guía (m)	*GHEE-ya*
guitar	guitarra	*ghee-TA-rra*

H

hair	cabello	*ka-BEL-yo*
hairbrush	cepillo	*seh-PEEL-yo*
haircut	corte de pelo	*KOR-teh deh PEH-lo*

half	mitad (f)	*mee-TAHD*
half (adj.)	medio	*MEHD-yo*
hand	mano (f)	*MA-no*
happy	feliz	*feh-LEESS*
harbor	puerto	*PWEHR-toh*
hard	duro	*DOO-ro*
hat	sombrero	*sohm-BREH-ro*
(to) have (possess)	tener	*teh-NEHR*
(I) have	tengo	*TEN-go*
(you sg.) have	(Ud.) tiene	*TYEH-neh*
(he, she) has	(él, ella) tiene	*TYEH-neh*
(we) have	tenemos	*teh-NEH-mohs*
(they, you pl.) have	(ellos, ellas, Uds.) tienen	*TYEH-nen*
Do you (sg.) have . . . ?	¿Tiene Ud. . . . ?	*¿TYEH-neh oo-STED . . . ?*
(to) have	haber	*ah-BEHR*

(Used to form the perfect tense; see p. 140.)

(I) have . . .	he . . .	*eh . . .*
(you sg.) have . . .	(Ud.) ha . . .	*ah . . .*
(he, she) has . . .	(él, ella) ha . . .	*ah . . .*
(we) have . . .	hemos. . .	*EH-mohs . . .*
(they, you pl.) have . . .	(ellos, ellas, Uds.) han . . .	*ahn . . .*

he	él	el
head	cabeza	ka-BEH-sa
(to) hear	oír	oh-EER
heart	corazón (m)	ko-ra-SOHN
heavy	pesado	peh-SA-doh
Hello!	¡Hola!	¡OH-la!
(to) help	ayudar	ah-yoo-DAR
Help!	¡Socorro!	¡so-KO-rro!
her (dir. obj.)	la	la
(to) her	le	leh
her (adj.)	su	soo
here	aquí	ah-KEE
hers	el suyo, la suya	el SOO-yo, la SOO-ya
herself (reflex.)	se	seh
high	alto	AHL-toh
highway	carretera	ka-rreh-TEH-ra
hill	colina	ko-LEE-na
him (dir. obj.)	lo, le	lo, leh
(to) him	le	leh
himself (reflex.)	se	seh
his (adj.)	su	soo
his (pron.)	el suyo, la suya	el SOO-yo, la SOO-ya
history	historia	ees-TOHR-ya
home	casa	KA-sa
(at) home	en casa	en KA-sa

Honduras	Honduras	*ohn-DOO-rahs*
Honduran	hondureño	*ohn-doo-REHN-yo*
horse	caballo	*ka-BAL-yo*
hospital	hospital (m)	*ohs-pee-TAHL*
hot	caliente	*ka-L'YEN-teh*
hotel	hotel (m)	*oh-TEL*
hour	hora	*OH-ra*
house	casa	*KA-sa*
how	como	*KO-mo*
however	sin embargo	*seen em-BAR-go*
hundred	cien	*s'yen*
a hundred (and)	ciento …	*S'YEN-toh …*
(to be) hungry	tener hambre	*teh-NEHR AHM-breh*
(to) hunt	cazar	*ka-SAHR*
(to) hurry	darse prisa	*DAR-seh PREE-sa*
Hurry up!	¡Dese prisa!	*¡DEH-seh PREE-sa!*
husband	esposo	*ess-PO-so*

I

I	yo	*yo*
ice	hielo	*YEH-lo*
ice cream	helado	*eh-LA-doh*
idiot	idiota (m)	*ee-D'YO-ta*
if	si	*see*
ill	enfermo	*en-FEHR-mo*

(to) import	importar	*eem-por-TAR*
important	importante	*eem-por-TAHN-teh*
impossible	imposible	*eem-po-SEE-bleh*
in	en	*en*
included	incluído	*een-kloo-EE-doh*
industry	industria	*een-DOOS-tree-ya*
information	información (f)	*een-for-ma-S'YOHN*
inhabitant	habitante (m)	*ah-bee-TAHN-teh*
inn	posada	*po-SA-da*
inquiry	pregunta	*preh-GOON-ta*
inside (direction)	adentro	*ah-DEN-tro*
inside (prep.)	dentro de	*DEN-tro deh*
instead	en vez de	*en vess deh*
intelligent	inteligente	*een-teh-lee-HEN-teh*
interested	interesado	*een-teh-reh-SA-doh*
interesting	interesante	*een-teh-reh-SAHN-teh*
interpreter	intérprete (m)	*een-TEHR-preh-teh*
into	dentro	*DEN-tro*
(to) introduce	presentar	*preh-sen-TAR*
invitation	invitación (f)	*een-vee-ta-S'YOHN*
is (permanent status)	es	*ess*
is (location or temporary status)	está	*ess-TA*
(there) is	hay	*1*

island	isla	*EES-la*
it (subject, or thing)	él (m), ella (f)	*el, EL-ya*
(subject, referring to an idea or situation)	ello	*EL-yo*
(object)	lo (m), la (f)	*lo, la*
(indirect object)	le	*leh*
its	su	*soo*
Israel	Israel	*ees-ra-EL*
Israeli	Israelí	*ees-ra-eh-LEE*
Italian	italiano	*ee-tahl-YA-no*
Italy	Italia	*ee-TAHL-ya*

J

jacket	chaqueta	*cha-KEH-ta*
jail	cárcel (f)	*KAR-sel*
January	enero	*eh-NEH-ro*
Japan	Japón	*ha-POHN*
Japanese	japonés	*ha-po-NEHS*
jewelry	joyas	*HO-yahs*
Jewish	judío	*hoo-DEE-yo*
job	empleo	*em-PLEH-oh*
joke	chiste (m)	*CHEES-teh*
July	julio	*HOOL-yo*

June	junio	*HOON-yo*
just (only)	solamente	*so-la-MEN-teh*
just now	ahora mismo .	*ah-OH-ra MEES-mo*

K

(to) keep	guardar	*gwahr-DAR*
Keep out!	¡No entre!	*¡no EN-treh!*
Keep quiet!	¡Cállese!	*¡KAHL-yeh-seh!*
key	llave (f)	*L'YA-veh*
kind (nice)	amable	*ah-MA-bleh*
kind (type)	tipo	*TEE-po*
king	rey	*ray*
kiss	beso	*BEH-so*
kitchen	cocina	*ko-SEE-na·*
knee	rodilla	*ro-DEEL-ya*
knife	cuchillo	*koo-CHEEL-yo*
(to) know (a person)	conocer	*ko-no-SEHR*
Do you know (a person) . . . ?	¿Conoce a . . . ?	*¿ko-NO-seh ah . . .*
(to) know (a fact or how to)	saber	*sa-BEHR*
Who knows?	¿Quién sabe?	*¿k'yen SA-beh?*

L

ladies' room	cuarto para señoras	KWAHR-toh PA-ra sen-YO-rahs
lady	dama	DA-ma
lake	lago	LA-go
lamb	cordero	kor-DEH-ro
land	tierra	T'YEH-rra
language	idioma (m)	ee-D'YO-ma
large	grande	GRAHN-deh
last	último	OOL-tee-mo
late	tarde	TAR-deh
later	más tarde	mahs TAR-deh
lawyer	abogado	ah-bo-GA-doh
(to) learn	aprender	ah-pren-DEHR
leather	cuero	KWEH-ro
(to) leave (something)	dejar	deh-HAR
(to) leave (depart)	salir	sa-LEER
left	izquierdo	ees-K'YEHR-doh
leg	pierna	P'YEHR-na
lemon	limón (m)	lee-MOHN
(to) lend	prestar	press-TAR
less	menos	MEH-nohs
lesson	lección (f)	lek-S'YOHN
let's	vamos a . . .	VA-mohs ah . . .

Let's go!	¡Vámonos!	¡VA-mo-nohs!
letter	carta	KAR-ta
lettuce	lechuga	leh-CHOO-ga
liberal	liberal	lee-beh-RAHL
liberty	libertad (f)	lee-behr-TAHD
lieutenant	teniente	ten-YEN-teh
life	vida	VEE-da
(to) lift	levantar	leh-vahn-TAR
light (weight)	liviano.	leev-YA-no
light (illumination)	luz (f)	looss
like	como	KO-mo
Like this.	Así.	ah-SEE
(to) like	gustar	goos-TAR

(See page 138 for usage.)

linen (material)	lino	LEE-no
lion	león	leh-OHN
lip	labio.	LAHB-yo
list	lista	LEES-ta
(to) listen	escuchar	es-koo-CHAR
Listen!	¡Escuche!	¡es-KOO-cheh!
little (small)	pequeño	peh-KEHN-yo
a little	un poco	oon PO-ko
(to) live	vivir	vee-VEER
lived	vivido	vee-VEE-doh

living room	sala	*SA-la*
lobster	langosta	*lahn-GOHS-ta*
long	largo	*LAR-go*
(to) look	mirar	*mee-RAR*
Look!	¡Mire!	*¡MEE-reh!*
Look out!	¡Cuidado!	*¡kwee-DA-doh!*
loose	flojo	*FLO-ho*
(to) lose	perder	*pehr-DEHR*
losses	perdidas	*PEHR-dee-dahs*
lost	perdido	*pehr-DEE-doh*
lot (much)	mucho	*MOO-cho*
(to) love	querer	*keh-REHR*
low	bajo	*BA-ho*
luck	suerte (f)	*SWEHR-teh*
Good luck!	¡Buena suerte!	*¡BWEH-na SWEHR-teh!*
luggage	equipaje (m)	*eh-kee-PA-heh*
lunch	almuerzo	*ahl-MWEHR-so*

M

machine	máquina	*MA-kee-na*
madam	señora	*sen-YO-ra*
made	hecho	*EH-cho*
maid	criada	*kree-AH-da*
mailbox	buzón (m)	*boo-SOHN*

(to) make	hacer	*ah-SEHR*
man	hombre	*OHM-breh*
manager	gerente	*heh-REN-teh*
many	muchos	*MOO-chohs*
map	mapa (m)	*MA-pa*
March	marzo	*MAR-so*
market	mercado	*mehr-KA-doh*
married	casado	*ka-SA-doh*
Mass (religious)	misa	*MEE-sa*
matches	fósforos	*FOHS-fo-rohs*
May	mayo	*MA-yo*
maybe	quizás	*kee-SAHS*
May I?	¿Se puede?	*¿seh PWEH-deh?*
me	me	*meh*
(to) mean	querer decir	*keh-REHR deh-SEER*
meat	carne (f)	*KAR-neh*
mechanic	mecánico	*meh-KA-nee-ko*
medicine	medicina	*meh-dee-SEE-na*
Mediterranean	Mediterráneo	*meh-dee-teh-RRA-neh-oh*
(to) meet (encounter)	encontrar	*en-kohn-TRAR*
meeting	reunión (f)	*reh-oon-YOHN*
member	miembro	*M'YEM-bro*
(to) mend	remendar	*reh-men-DAR*

men's room	cuarto para caballeros	KWAHR-toh PA-ra ka-bahl-YEH-rohs
menu	menú	meh-NOO
message	mensaje (m)	men-SA-heh
meter (39.37 inches, slightly more than a yard)	metro	MEH-tro
Mexico	México	MEH-hee-ko
Mexican	Mexicano	meh-hee-KA-no
middle	medio	MEHD-yo
might See "could."		
mile	milla	MEEL-ya
milk	leche (f)	LEH-cheh
million	millón (m)	meel-YOHN
mine	el mío, la mía	el MEE-yo, la MEE-ya
mineral water	agua mineral	AH-gwa mee-neh-RAHL
minister	ministro	mee-NEESS-tro
minute	minuto	mee-NOO-toh
Miss	señorita	sen-yo-REE-ta
(to) miss (the train, etc.)	perder	pehr-DEHR
(to) miss (sentiment)	echar de menos	eh-CHAR deh MEH-nohs
mistake	error (m)	eh-RROR

misunderstand-ing	malentendido	*mahl-en-ten-DEE-doh*
model	modelo (m or f)	*mo-DEH-lo*
modern	moderno	*mo-DEHR-no*
moment	momento	*mo-MEN-toh*
Monday	lunes	*LOO-ness*
money	dinero	*dee-NEH-ro*
monkey	mono	*MO-no*
month	mes (m)	*mess*
monument	monumento	*mo-noo-MEN-toh*
moon	luna	*LOO-na*
more	más	*mahs*
morning	mañana	*mahn-YA-na*
mosquito	mosquito	*mohs-KEE-toh*
most	la mayor parte	*la ma-YOR PAR-teh*
mother	madre (f)	*MA-dreh*
mother-in-law	suegra	*SWEH-gra*
motor	motor (m)	*mo-TOR*
motorcycle	motocicleta	*mo-toh-see-KLEH-ta*
mountain	montaña	*mohn-TAHN-ya*
mouse	ratón (m)	*ra-TOHN*
mouth	boca	*BO-ka*
movie	película	*peh-LEE-koo-la*
movies	cine (m)	*SEE-neh*
Mr.	señor (Sr.)	*sen-YOR*

Mrs.	señora (Sra.)	*sen-YO-ra*
much	mucho	*MOO-cho*
museum	museo	*moo-SEH-oh*
music	música	*MOO-see-ka*
musician	músico	*MOO-see-ko*
must	hay que	*I keh*
(I, you, he, etc.) must go	hay que ir	*I keh eer*
mustache	bigote (m)	*bee-GO-teh*
mustard	mostaza	*mohs-TA-sa*
my	mi	*mee*
myself (reflex.)	me	*meh*

N

name	nombre (m)	*NOHM-breh*
napkin	servilleta	*sehr-veel-YEH-ta*
narcotics	narcóticos	*nar-KO-tee-kohs*
narrow	angosto	*ahn-GOHS-toh*
navy	marina	*ma-REE-na*
near	cerca	*SEHR-ka*
necessary	necesario	*neh-seh-SAR-yo*
neck	cuello	*KWEL-yo*
necktie	corbata	*kor-BA-ta*
(to) need	necesitar	*neh-seh-see-TAR*
neighborhood	vecindario	*veh-seen-DAR-yo*

nephew	sobrino	*so-BREE-no*
nervous	nervioso	*nehr-V'YO-so*
neutral	neutral	*neh-oo-TRAHL*
never	nunca	*NOON-ka*
Never mind.	No importa.	*nò eem-POR-ta.*
new	nuevo	*NWEH-vo*
news	noticias	*no-TEE-s'yahs*
newspaper	periódico	*pehr-YO-dee-ko*
New Year	Año Nuevo	*AHN-yo NWEH-vo*
next	próximo	*PROHX-see-mo*
Nicaragua	Nicaragua	*nee-ka-RA-gwa*
Nicaraguan	nicaragüense	*nee-ka-ra-GWEN-seh*
nice	simpático	*seem-PA-tee-ko*
niece	sobrina	*so-BREE-na*
night	noche (f)	*NO-cheh*
nightclub	club nocturno	*kloob nohk-TOOR-no*
nightgown	camisa de dormir	*ka-MEE-sa deh dor-MEER*
nine	nueve	*NWEH-veh*
nineteen	diecinueve	*d'yess-ee-NWEH-veh*
ninety	noventa	*no-VEN-ta*
no	no	*no*
nobody	nadie	*NAHD-yeh*
noise	ruido	*RWEE-doh*
none	ninguno	*neen-GOO-no*

noon	mediodía (m)	*meh-d'yo-DEE-ya*
normal	normal	*nor-MAHL*
north	norte	*NOR-teh*
nose	nariz (f)	*na-REES*
not	no	*no*
not yet	todavía no	*to-da-VEE-ya no*
nothing	nada	*NA-da*
(to) notice	notar	*no-TAR*
noun	nombre (m)	*NOHM-breh*
November	noviembre	*no-V'YEM-breh*
now	ahora	*ah-OH-ra*
nowhere	en ninguna parte	*en neen-GOO-na PAR-teh*
number	número	*NOO-meh-ro*
nurse	enfermera	*en-fehr-MEH-ra*
nuts	nueces (f)	*NWEH-sehs*

O

occasionally	de vez en cuando	*deh vehs en KWAHN-doh*
occupied	ocupado	*oh-koo-PA-doh*
ocean	océano	*oh-SEH-ah-no*
o'clock (See page 32 for usage.)		
October	octubre	*ohk-TOO-breh*
of	de	*·deh*

(to) offer	ofrecer	*oh-freh-SEHR*
office	oficina	*oh-fee-SEE-na*
officer	oficial	*oh-fees-YAHL*
often	a menudo	*ah meh-NOO-doh*
oil	aceite (m)	*ah-SAY-teh*
O.K.	está bien	*ess-TA b'yen*
old	viejo	*V'YEH-ho*
olive	aceituna	*ah-say-TOO-na*
omelet	tortilla de huevos	*tor-TEEL-ya deh WEH-vohs*
on	sobre	*SO-breh*
once	una vez	*OO-na vess*
At once!	¡En seguida!	*¡en seh-GHEE-da!*
one	uno ·	*OO-no*
one way (traffic)	una vía	*OO-na VEE-ya*
one way (ticket)	ida	*EE-da*
on time	a tiempo	*ah T'YEM-po*
onion	cebolla	*seh-BOHL-ya*
only	solamente	*so-la-MEN-teh*
open	abierto	*ah-B'YEHR-toh*
(to) open	abrir	*ah-BREER*
opera	ópera	*OH-peh-ra*
opinion	·opinión (f)	*oh-peen-YOHN*
opportunity	oportunidad (f)	*oh-por-too-nee-DAHD*

opposite	opuesto	oh-PWESS-toh
or	o	oh
orange	naranja	na-RAHN-ha
orchestra	orquesta	or-KESS-ta
order	orden (f)	OR-den
(to) order	ordenar	or-deh-NAR
in order to	para	PA-ra
original	original	oh-ree-hee-NAHL
other	otro	OH-tro
ought to (I, you sg., he, she) ought to	debería (yo, Ud. él, élla)	deh-beh-REE-ya
(we) ought to	deberíamos	deh-beh-REE-ya-mohs
(they, you pl.) ought to	(ellos, ellas, Uds.) deberían	deh-beh-REE-yahn
our	nuestro	NWESS-tro
ours	el nuestro, la nuestra	el NWESS-tro, la NWESS-tra
ourselves (reflex.)	nos	nohs
outside	afuera	ah-FWEH-ra
over	encima	en-SEE-ma
overcoat	abrigo	ah-BREE-go
over there	allá	ahl-YA
overweight	sobrepeso	so-breh-PEH-so

(to) owe	deber	*deh-BEHR*
own	propio	*PRO-p'yo*
owner	dueño	*DWEN-yo*
ox	buey (m)	*bway*
oyster	ostra	*OHS-tra*

P

package	paquete (m)	*pa-KEH-teh*
paid	pagado	*pa-GA-doh*
pain	dolor (m)	*doh-LOR*
(to) paint	pintar	*peen-TAR*
painting	cuadro	*KWA-dro*
palace	palacio	*pa-LA-s'yo*
pan	cacerola	*ka-seh-RO-la*
Panama	Panamá	*pa-na-MA*
Panamanian	panameño	*pa-na-MEN-yo*
paper	papel (m)	*pa-PEL*
parade	desfile (m)	*des-FEE-leh*
Paraguay	Paraguay	*pa-ra-G'WY*
Paraguayan	paraguayo	*pa-ra-GWA-yo*
Pardon me!	¡Perdón!	*¡pehr-DOHN!*
park	parque (m)	*PAR-keh*
(to) park	estacionar	*ess-ta-s'yo-NAR*
parents	padres	*PA-drehs*
part	parte (f)	*PAR-teh*

participle	participio	*par-tee-SEEP-yo*
partner	socio	*SOHS-yo*
party	fiesta	*F'YES-ta*
passenger	pasajero	*pa-sa-HEH-ro*
passport	pasaporte (m)	*pa-sa-POR-teh*
past	pasado	*pa-SA-doh*
past tense	tiempo pasado	*TYEM-po pa-SA-doh*
(to) pay	pagar	*pa-GAR*
(to) pay cash	pagar al con-	*pa-GAR ahl*
	tado	*kohn-TA-doh*
peace	paz (f)	*pahss*
pen	pluma	*PLOO-ma*
pencil	lápiz (m)	*LA-peess*
people	gente (f)	*HEN-teh*
percent	por ciento	*por S'YEN-toh*
perfect	perfecto	*pehr-FEK-toh*
perfume	perfume (m)	*pehr-FOO-meh*
perhaps	quizás	*kee-SAHS*
permanent	permanente	*pehr-ma-NEN-teh*
(to) permit	permitir	*pehr-mee-TEER*
permitted	permitido	*pehr-mee-TEE-doh*
person	persona	*pehr-SO-na*
Peru	Perú (m)	*peh-ROO*
Peruvian	Peruano	*peh-RWA-no*
Philippines	Filipinas	*fee-lee-PEE-nahs*

phone	teléfono	*teh-LEH-fo-no*
photo	foto (f)	*FO-toh*
piano	piano	*P'YA-no*
(to) pick up	recoger	*reh-ko-HEHR*
picture	retrato	*reh-TRA-toh*
piece	pedazo	*peh-DA-so*
pier	muelle (m)	*MWEL-yeh*
pill	píldora	*PEEL-doh-ra*
pillow	almohada	*ahl-mo-AH-da*
pin	alfiler (m)	*ahl-fee-LEHR*
pink	rosado	*ro-SA-doh*
pipe .	pipa	*PEE-pa*
pistol ·	pistola	*pees-TOH-la*
place	lugar (m)	*loo-GAR*
plain (simple)	sencillo	*sen-SEEL-yo*
plan	plan (m)	*plahn*
plane	avión (m)	*ahv-YOHN*
planet	planeta (m)	*pla-NEH-ta*
plant (garden)	planta	*PLAHN-ta*
plant (factory)	fábrica	*FA-bree-ka*
plate	plato	*PLA-toh*
play (theater)	pieza	*P'YEH-sa*
(to) play	jugar	*hoo-GAR*
plastic	plástico	*PLAHS-tee-ko*
pleasant	agradable	*ah-gra-DA-bleh*

please	por favor	*por fa-VOR*
pleasure	placer (m)	*pla-SEHR*
plural	plural (m)	*ploo-RAHL*
pocket	bolsillo	*bol-SEEL-yo*
poetry	poesía	*po-eh-SEE-ya*
(to) point	señalar	*sen-ya-LAHR*
poisonous	venenoso	*veh-neh-NO-so*
police	policía (f)	*po-lee-SEE-ya*
policeman	policía (m)	*po-lee-SEE-ya*
police station	cuartel de · policía (m)	*kwahr-TEL deh po-lee-SEE-ya*
polite	cortés	*kor-TEHS*
poor	pobre	*PO-breh*
pope	papa (m)	*PA-pa*
popular	popular	*po-poo-LAR*
pork	cerdo	*SEHR-doh*
Portugal	Portugal	*por-too-GAHL*
Portuguese	portugués	*por-too-GAYSS*
possible	posible	*po-SEE-bleh*
postcard	tarjeta postal	*tar-HEH-ta pos-TAHL*
post office	correo	*ko-RREH-oh*
potato	papa	*PA-pa*
pound	libra	*LEE-bra*
(to) practice	practicar	*prahk-tee-KAR*
(to) prefer	preferir	*preh-feh-REER*

pregnant	embarazada	*em-ba-ra-SA-da*
(to) prepare	preparar	*preh-pa-RAR*
present (time)	presente	*preh-SEN-teh*
present (gift)	regalo	*reh-GA-lo*
president	presidente (m)	*preh-see-DEN-teh*
(to) press (clothes)	planchar	*plahn-CHAR*
pretty	bonito	*bo-NEE-toh*
previously	previamente	*prehv-ya-MEN-teh*
price	precio	*PRESS-yo*
priest	sacerdote	*sa-sehr-DOH-teh*
prince	príncipe	*PREEN-see-peh*
princess	princesa	*preen-SEH-sa*
principal	principal	*preen-see-PAHL*
prison	cárcel (f)	*KAR-sel*
private	privado	*pree-VA-doh*
probably	probablemente	*pro-ba-bleh-MEN-teh*
problem	problema (m)	*pro-BLEH-ma*
production	producción (f)	*pro-dook-S'YOHN*
profession	profesión (f)	*pro-feh-S'YOHN*
professor	profesor (m)	*pro-feh-SOR*
profits	beneficios	*beh-neh-FEE-s'yohs*
program	programa (m)	*pro-GRA-ma*
(to) promise	prometer	*pro-meh-TEHR*
promised	prometido	*pro-meh-TEE-doh*

pronoun	pronombre (m)	*pro-NOHM-breh*
(to) pronounce	pronunciar	*pro-noon-S'YAR*
propaganda	propaganda	*pro-pa-GAHN-da*
property	propiedad (f)	*prop-yeh-DAHD*
Protestant	protestante	*pro-tess-TAHN-teh*
public	público	*POO-blee-ko*
publicity	publicidad (f)	*poo-blee-see-DAHD*
publisher	editor (m)	*eh-dee-TOR*
(to) pull	tirar	*tee-RAR*
(to) purchase	comprar	*kohm-PRAR*
pure	puro	*POO-ro*
purple	morado	*mo-RA-doh*
purse	cartera	*kar-TEH-ra*
(to) push	empujar	*em-poo-HAR*
(to) put	poner	*po-NEHR*
(to) put on	ponerse	*po-NEHR-seh*

Q

quality	calidad (f)	*ka-lee-DAHD*
queen	reina	*RAY-na*
question	pregunta	*preh-GOON-ta*
quick	rápido	*RA-pee-doh*
quickly	rápidamente	*RA-pee-da-MEN-teh*
quiet	callado	*kahl-YA-doh*
quite	bastante	*ba-STAHN-teh*

R

rabbi	rabino	*ra-BEE-no*
rabbit	conejo	*ko-NEH-jo*
race (contest)	carrera	*ka-RREH-ra*
race (ethnic)	raza	*RA-sa*
radio	radio	*RAH-d'yo*
railroad	ferrocarril (m)	*feh-rro-ka-RREEL*
rain	lluvia	*L'YOOV-ya*
It's raining.	Está lloviendo.	*ess-TA l'yo-V'YEN-doh*
raincoat	impermeable (m)	*eem-pehr-meh-AH-bleh*
rapidly	rápidamente	*RA-pee-da-MEN-teh*
rarely	rara vez	*RA-ra vess*
rate	cantidad (f)	*kahn-tee-DAHD*
rather	más bien	*mahs b'yen*
(I, he, she, you, sg.) would rather	preferiría	*preh-feh-ree-REE-ya*
razor	navaja de afeitar	*na-VA-ha deh ah-fay-TAR*
(to) read	leer.	*leh-EHR*
ready	listo	*LEES-toh*
really	verdaderamente	*vehr-da-deh-ra-MEN-teh*
reason	razón (f)	*ra-SOHN*
receipt	recibo	*reh-SEE-bo*

(to) receive	recibir	*reh-see-BEER*
recently	recientemente	*rehs-yen-teh-MEN-teh*
recipe	receta	*reh-SEH-ta*
(to) recognize	reconocer	*reh-ko-no-SEHR*
(to) recommend	recomendar	*reh-ko-men-DAR*
red	rojo	*RO-ho*
refrigerator	nevera	*neh-VEH-ra*
(to) refuse	rehusar	*reh-oo-SAR*
(My) regards to . . .	(Mis) recuerdos a . . .	*meess reh-KWER-dohs ah . . .*
regular	regular	*reh-goo-LAR*
religion	religión (f)	*reh-lee-H'YOHN*
(to) remain	quedarse	*keh-DAR-seh*
(to) remember	recordar	*reh-kor-DAR*
(to) rent	alquilar	*ahl-kee-LAR*
(to) repair	reparar	*reh-pa-RAR*
(to) repeat	repetir	*reh-peh-TEER*
Repeat, please!	¡Repita, por favor!	*¡reh-PEE-ta, por fa-VOR!*
report	reporte (m)	*reh-POR-teh*
(to) represent	representar	*reh-preh-sen-TAR*
representative	representante (m)	*reh-preh-sen-TAHN-teh*
resident (m or f)	residente	*reh-see-DEN-teh*
responsible	responsable	*rehs-pohn-SA-bleh*
rest (remainder)	resto	*RESS-toh*

(to) rest	descansar	*des-kahn-SAR*
restaurant	restaurante (m)	*rest-ow-RAHN-teh*
(to) return (to a place)	regresar	*reh-greh-SAR*
(to) return (give back)	devolver	*deh-vohl-VEHR*
revolution	revolución (f)	*reh-vo-loo-S'YOHN*
reward	recompensa	*reh-kohm-PEN-sa*
rice	arroz (m)	*ah-RROHS*
rich	rico	*REE-ko*
(to) ride (a horse, bicycle, etc.) (See page 138 for use.)	montar a	*mohn-TAR ah*
right (direction)	derecho	*deh-REH-cho*
to the right	a la derecha	*ah lah deh-REH-cha*
right (correct)	correcto	*ko-RREK-toh*
You're right.	Tiene razón.	*T'YEH-neh ra-SOHN.*
Right away!	¡En seguida!	*¡en seh-GHEE-da!*
ring	anillo	*ah-NEEL-yo*
riot	motín (m)	*mo-TEEN*
river	río	*REE-yo*
road	camino	*ka-MEE-no*
roof	techo	*TEH-cho*
room	cuarto	*KWAHR-toh*
room (space)	espacio	*eh-SPA-s'yo*

room service	servicio de comedor	*sehr-VEE-s'yo deh ko-meh-DOR*
round trip	ida y vuelta	*EE-da ee VWEL-ta*
route	ruta	*ROO-ta*
rug	alfombra	*ahl-FOHM-bra*
(to) run	correr	*ko-RREHR*
Run!	¡Corra!	*¡KO-rral*
Russia	Rusia	*ROO-s'ya*
Russian	ruso	*ROO-so*

S

sad	triste	*TREESS-teh*
safe (adj.)	seguro	*seh-GOO-ro*
safety pin	imperdible (m)	*eem-pehr-DEE-bleh*
said	dicho	*DEE-cho*
sailor	marinero	*ma-ree-NEH-ro*
saint · (Generally shortened to *San* before masculine names.)	santo (m), santa (f)	*SAHN-toh, SAHN-ta*
salad	ensalada	*en-sa-LA-da*
salary	sueldo	*SWEL-doh*
sale	venta	*VEN-ta*
Salvador	Salvador	*sahl-va-DOR*
Salvadorian	salvadoreño	*sahl-va-doh-REHN-yo*

same	mismo	MEES-mò
sandwich	emparedado	em-pa-reh-DA-doh
Saturday	sábado	SA-ba-doh
(to) say	decir	deh-SEER
scenery	paisaje (m)	py-SA-heh
school	escuela	ess-KWEH-la
scissors	tijeras	tee-HEH-rahs
Scotch	escocés	ess-ko-SESS
Scotland	Escocia	ess-KO-s'ya
sea	mar (m)	mar
seafood	mariscos	ma-REES-kohs
season	estación (f)	ess-ta-S'YOHN
seat	asiento	ah-S'YEN-toh
secretary	secretaria (f)	seh-kreh-TAR-ya
(to) see	ver	vehr
(to) seem	parecer	pa-reh-SEHR
It seems ...	Parece ...	pa-REH-seh ...
seen	visto	VEES-toh
seldom	rara vez	RA-ra vess
self (my, you, him, her)	(yo, Ud., él, ella) mismo	MEESS-mo
(to) sell	vender	ven-DEHR
(to) send	mandar	mahn-DAR
(to) send for	enviar por	en-vee-AR por
separate	separado	seh-pa-RA-doh
September	septiembre	sep-T'YEM-breh

serious	serio	SEHR-yo
service	servicio	sehr-VEE-s'yo
seven	siete	S'YEH-teh
seventeen	diecisiete	d'yess-ee-S'YEH-teh
seventy	setenta	seh-TEN-ta
several	varios	VAR-yohs
shall		
(See "will.")		
shampoo	shampú (m)	shahm-POO
shark	tiburón (m)	tee-boo-ROHN
sharp	agudo	ah-GOO-doh
she	ella	EL-ya
ship	barco	BAR-ko
shipment	envío	en-VEE-yo
shirt	camisa	ka-MEE-sa
shoe	zapato	sa-PA-toh
shop	tienda	TYEN-da
short	corto	KOR-toh
should	deber	deh-BEHR

(Use the appropriate forms of *deber* with the infinitive.)

(I, you, sg., he, she) should	debería	deh-beh-REE-ya
(we) should	deberíamos	deh-beh-REE-ya-mohs
(they, you pl.) should	deberían	deh-beh-REE-yahn

shoulder	hombro	*OHM-bro*
show	espectáculo	*ess-pek-TA-koo-lo*
(to) show	mostrar	*mohs-TRAR*
Show me?	¡Muéstreme!	*¡MWESS-treh-meh!*
shower	ducha	*DOO-cha*
shrimps	camarones (m)	*ka-ma-RO-nehs*
shut	cerrado	*seh-RRA-doh*
(to) shut	cerrar	*seh-RRAR*
sick	enfermo	*en-FEHR-mo*
(to) sign	firmar	*feer-MAR*
silk	seda	*SEH-da*
silver	plata	*PLA-ta*
simple	sencillo	*sen-SEEL-yo*
since	desde	*DEHS-deh*
sincerely	sinceramente	*seen-seh-ra-MEN-teh*
(to) sing	cantar	*kahn-TAR*
singer (m or f)	cantante	*kahn-TAHN-teh*
sir	señor	*sen-YOR*
sister	hermana	*ehr-MA-na*
sister-in-law	cuñada	*koon-YA-da*
(to) sit down	sentarse	*sen-TAR-seh*
Sit down?	¡Siéntese!	*¡S'YEN-teh-seh!*
six	seis	*sayss*
sixteen	dieciseis	*d'yess-ee-SAYSS*
sixty	sesenta	*seh-SEN-ta*

size	tamaño	*ta-MAHN-yo*
(to) skate	patinar	*pa-tee-NAR*
(to) ski	esquiar	*ess-kee-AR*
skin	piel (f)	*p'yell*
skirt	falda	*FAHL-da*
sky	cielo	*S'YEH-lo*
(to) sleep	dormir	*dor-MEER*
sleeve	manga	*MAHN-ga*
slowly	despacio	*dess-PA-s'yo*
small	pequeño	*peh-KEN-yo*
smoke	humo	*OO-mo*
(to) smoke	fumar	*foo-MAR*
snow	nieve (f)	*N'YEH-veh*
so	así	*ah-SEE*
soap	jabón (m)	*ha-BOHN*
sock	media	*MEHD-ya*
sofa	sofá (m)	*so-FA*
soft	blando	*BLAHN-doh*
soldier	soldado	*sol-DA-doh*
some (pron.)	un poco de	*oon PO-ko deh*
some (adj.)	algunos	*ahl-GOO-nohs*
somebody	alguien	*AHL-g'yen*
something	algo	*AHL-go*
something else	algo más	*AHL-go mahs*

sometimes	algunas veces	*ahl-GOO-nahs VEH-sehs*
somewhere	en alguna parte	*en ahl-GOO-na PAR-teh*
son	hijo	*EE-ho*
son-in-law	yerno	*YEHR-no*
song	canción (f)	*kahn-S'YOHN*
soon	pronto	*PROHN-toh*
(I am) sorry.	Lo siento.	*lo S'YEN-toh*
soup	sopa	*SO-pa*
south	sur	*soor*
South America	Sur América	*soor ah-MEH-ree-ka*
South American	Suramérícano	*soor-ah-meh-ree-KA-no*
souvenir	recuerdo	*reh-KWER-doh*
Spain	España	*ess-PAHN-ya*
Spanish, Spaniard	español	*ess-pahn-YOHL*
(to) speak	hablar	*ah-BLAR*
special	especial	*ess-peh-S'YAHL*
(to) spend	gastar	*gahs-TAR*
spoon	cuchara	*koo-CHA-ra*
sport	deporte (m)	*deh-POR-teh*
spring (season)	primavera	*pree-ma-VEH-ra*
stairs	escalera	*ess-ka-LEH-ra*
stamp	estampilla	*ess-tahm-PEEL-ya*

star	estrella	*ess-TREL-ya*
(to) start	empezar	*em-peh-SAR*
state	estado	*ess-TA-doh*
station.	estación (f)	*ess-ta-S'YOHN*
status	estatua	*ess-TA-twah*
(to) stay	quedarse	*keh-DAR-seh*
steak	bistec (m)	*beess-TEK*
steel	acero	*ah-SEH-ro*
stewardess	aeromoza	*ah-eh-ro-MO-sa*
still (adv.)	todavía	*toh-da-VEE-ya*
stocking	media	*MEHD-ya*
stockmarket	bolsa	*BOHL-sa*
stocks (shares)	acciones	*ahk-S'YOH-nehs*
stone	piedra	*P'YEH-dra*
Stop!	¡Pare!	*¡PA-reh!*
Stop it!	¡Deje de hacer eso!	*DEH-heh deh ah-SEHR EH-so!*
store	tienda	*T'YEN-da*
storm	tormenta	*tor-MEN-ta*
story	cuento	*KWEN-toh*
straight or straight ahead	derecho	*deh-REH-cho*
strange	extraño	*es-TRAHN-yo*
street	calle (f)	*KAHL-yeh*
string	cuerda	*KWER-da*

strong	fuerte	FWEHR-teh
student (m or f)	estudiante	ess-too-D'YAHN-teh
(to) study	estudiar	ess-too-D'YAR
style	estilo	ess-TEE-lo
subway	metro, sub-terráneo (in Spain)	MEH-tro, soob-teh-RRA-neh-yo
suddenly	de repente	deh reh-PEN-teh
suede	gamuza	ga-MOO-sa
sugar	azúcar (f)	ah-SOO-kar
suit (clothes)	traje (m)	TRA-heh
suitcase	maleta	ma-LEH-ta
summer	verano	veh-RA-no
sun	sol (m)	sohl
Sunday	domingo	do-MEEN-go
sure	seguro	seh-GOO-ro
surely	seguramente	seh-goo-ra-MEN-teh
surprise	sorpresa	sor-PREH-sa
sweater	suéter (m)	SWEH-tehr
sweet	dulce	DOOL-seh
(to) swim	nadar	na-DAR
swimming pool	piscina	pee-SEE-na
Swiss	suizo	SWEE-so
Switzerland	Suiza	SWEE-sa

T

tablecloth	mantel (m)	*mahn-TEL*
tailor	sastre (m)	*SAHS-treh*
(to) take	tomar	*toh-MAR*
(to) take away	llevarse	*l'yeh-VAR-seh*
(to) take a walk (or a ride)	dar un paseo	*dar oon pa-SEH-oh*
(to) talk	hablar	*ah-BLAR*
tall	alto	*AHL-toh*
tank	tanque (m)	*TAHN-keh*
tape	cinta	*SEEN-ta*
tape recorder	grabador (m)	*gra-ba-DOR*
tax	impuesto	*eem-PWESS-toh*
taxi	taxi (m)	*TAHX-see*
tea	té (m)	*teh*
(to) teach	enseñar	*en-sen-YAR*
teacher	maestro	*ma-ESS-tro*
team	equipo	*eh-KEE-po*
telegram	telegrama (m)	*teh-leh-GRA-ma*
telephone	teléfono	*teh-LEH-fo-no*
television	televisión (f)	*teh-leh-vee-S'YOHN*
(to) tell	decir	*deh-SEER*
Tell him (her) that . . .	Dígale que . . .	*DEE-ga-leh keh . . .*
temperature	temperatura	*tem-peh-ra-TOO-ra*
temple	templo	*TEM-plo*

ten	diez	*d'yess*
tennis	tenis (m)	*TEH-neess*
terrace	terraza	*teh-RRA-sa*
terrible	terrible	*teh-RREE-bleh*
than (Before a number use *de*.)	que	*keh*
Thank you.	Gracias.	*GRA-s'yahs.*
that (pron.)	ése (m), ésa (f)	*ESS-eh, ESS-ah*
that (neut.)	eso	*ES-so*
that (adj.)	ese, esa	*ESS-eh, ESS-ah*
that (rel. pron. or conj.)	que	*keh*
the	el (m)	*el*
	la (f)	*lah*
	los (m. pl.)	*lohs*
	las (f. pl.)	*lahs*
their	su	*soo*
theirs	el suyo (m), la suya (f)	*el SOO-yo, la SOO-ya*
them	los (m), las (f)	*lohs, lahs*
themselves (reflex.)	se	*seh*
then	entonces	*en-TOHN-sess*
there	allí	*ahl-YEE*
There is . . .	Hay . . .	*I*
There are . . .	Hay . . .	*I*
these (pronoun)	éstos (m), éstas (f)	*ESS-tohs, ESS-tahs*

these (adjective)	estos (m), estas (f)	ESS-tohs, ESS-tahs
they	ellos (m), ellas (f)	EL-yohs, EL-yahs
thin	delgado	del-GA-doh
thing	cosa	KO-sa
(to) think	pensar	pen-SAR
Do you think that . . . ?	¿Piensa Ud. que . . . ?	¿P'YEN-sa oo-STED keh . . . ?
I think	Pienso que . . .	P'YEN-so keh . . .
third	tercero	tehr-SEH-ro
(to be) thirsty	tener sed	teh-NEHR sed
thirteen	trece	TREH-seh
thirty	treinta	TRAIN-ta
this (pron.)	éste (m), ésta (f)	ESS-teh, ESS-tah
this (adj.)	este (m), esta (f)	ESS-teh, ESS-ta
those (pron.)	ésos (m), ésas (f)	ESS-ohs, ESS-ahs
those (adj.)	esos (m), esas (f)	ESS-ohs, ESS-ahs
thousand	mil	meel
thread	hilo	EE-lo
three	tres	trehs
throat	garganta	gahr-GAHN-ta
through	por	por

Thursday	jueves	*HWEH-vehs*
ticket	billete (m)	*beel-YEH-teh*
tie	corbata	*kor-BA-ta*
tiger	tigre (m)	*TEE-greh*
time	tiempo	*T'YEM-po*
tip	propina	*pro-PEE-na*
tire	llanta	*L'YAHN-ta*
tired	cansado	*kahn-SA-doh*
to (direction)	a	*ah*
to (in order to)	para	*PA-ra*
tobacco	tabaco	*ta-BA-ko*
today	hoy	*oy*
toe	dedo del pie	*DEH-do del p'yeh*
together	juntos	*HOON-tohs*
tomato	tomate (m)	*toh-MA-teh*
tomb	tumba	*TOOM-ba*
tongue	lengua	*LEN-gwa*
tonight	esta noche	*ESS-ta NO-cheh*
too (also)	también	*tahm-B'YEN*
too (excessive)	demasiado	*deh-ma-S'YA-doh*
tool	herramienta	*eh-rra-M'YEN-ta*
tooth (front)	diente (m)	*D'YEN-teh*
tooth (molar)	muela	*MWEH-la*
toothbrush	cepillo de dientes	*seh-PEEL-yo deh D'YEN-tehs*

toothpaste	pasta de dientes	*PAHS-ta deh. D'YEN-tehs*
tour	jira	*HEE-ra*
tourist (m or f)	turista	*too-REESS-ta*
toward	hacia	*AHS-ya*
towel	toalla	*toh-AHL-ya*
tower	torre (f)	*TOH-rreh*
town	pueblo	*PWEH-blo*
toy	juguete (m)	*hoo-GHEH-teh*
traffic	tráfico	*TRA-fee-ko*
train	tren (m)	*trehn*
translation	traducción (f)	*tra-dook-S'YOHN*
(to) travel	viajar	*v'ya-HAR*
travel agent	agente de viajes	*ah-HEN-teh deh V'YA-hehs*
traveler	viajero	*v'ya-HEH-ro*
treasurer	tesorero	*teh-so-REH-ro*
tree	árbol (m)	*AR-bohl*
trip	viaje (m)	*V'YA-heh*
trouble	problema (m)	*pro-BLEH-ma*
trousers	pantalones (m)	*pahn-ta-LO-nehs*
truck	camión (m)	*kah-M'YOHN*
true	verdad	*vehr-DAHD*
truth	verdad (f)	*vehr-DAHD*
(to) try	tratar	*tra-TAR*

(to) try on	probarse	pro-BAR-seh
Tuesday	martes	MAR-tehs
Turkey	Turquía	toor-KEE-ya
Turkish	turko	TOOR-ko
(to) turn	voltear	vohl-teh-AR
(to) turn off	apagar	ah-pa-GAR
(to) turn on	poner	po-NEHR
twelve	doce	DOH-seh
twenty	veinte	VAIN-teh
two	dos	dohs
typewriter	máquina de escribir	MA-kee-na deh ess-kree-BEER
typical	típico	TEE-pee-ko

U

ugly	feo	FEH-oh
umbrella	paraguas (m)	pa-RA-gwahs
uncle	tío	TEE-yo
under	debajo de	deh-BA-ho deh
underneath	debajo	deh-BA-ho
understand	comprender	kohm-pren-DEHR
Do you understand?	¿Comprende Ud.?	¿kohm-PREN-deh oo-STED?
I don't understand.	No comprendo.	no kohm-PREN-doh.
underwear	ropa interior	RO-pa een-TEHR-YOR

unfortunately	desafortuna- damente	*dehs-ah-for-too- na-da-MEN-teh*
uniform	uniforme (m)	*oo-nee-FOR-meh*
United Nations	Naciones Uni- das	*na-S'YO-ness oo-NEE-dahs*
United States	Estados Uni- dos	*ess-TA-dohs oo-NEE-dohs*
university	universidad (f)	*oo-nee-vehr- see-DAHD*
until	hasta	*AHS-ta*
up	arriba	*ah-RREE-ba*
urgent	urgente	*oor-HEN-teh*
Uruguay	Uruguay (m)	*oo-roo-G'WY*
Uruguayan	uruguayo	*oo-roo-GWA-yo*
us	nos	*nohs*
(to) use	usar	*oo-SAR*
used to (in the habit of)	acostumbrado a	*ah-kohs-toom- BRA-doh ah*
useful	útil	*OO-teel*
usually	usualmente	*oo-swahl-MEN-teh*

V

vacant	desocupado	*dehs-oh-koo-PA-doh*
vacation	vacación (f)	*va-ka-S'YOHN*
vaccination	vacuna	*va-KOO-na*
valley	valle (m)	*VAHL-yeh*
valuable	valioso	*va-L'YO-so*

value	valor (m)	*va-LOR*
vanilla	vainilla	*vy-NEEL-ya*
various	varios	*VAR-yohs*
vegetable	legumbre (m)	*leh-GOOM-breh*
Venezuela	Venezuela	*veh-neh-SWEH-la*
Venezuelan	venezolano	*veh-neh-so-LA-no*
verb	verbo	*VEHR-bo*
very	muy	*mwee*
very well	muy bien	*mwee b'yen*
view	vista	*VEESS-ta*
village	aldea	*ahl-DEH-ah*
vinegar	vinagre (m)	*vee-NA-greh*
violin	violín (m)	*v'yo-LEEN*
visa	visa	*VEE-sa*
visit	visita	*vee-SEE-ta*
(to) visit	visitar	*vee-see-TAR*
vivid	vívido	*VEE-vee-doh*
voice	voz (f)	*vohs*
volcano	volcán (m)	*vohl-KAHN*
voyage	viaje (m)	*V'YA-heh*

W

waist	cintura	*seen-TOO-ra*
(to) wait	esperar	*ess-peh-RAR*
Wait here!	¡Espere aquí!	*¡ess-PEH-reh ah-KEE!*

waiter	camarero, moso	*ka-ma-REH-ro, MO-so*
waitress	camarera, mosa	*ka-ma-REH-ra, MO-sa*
(to) walk	caminar	*ka-mee-NAR*
wall	pared (f)	*pa-RED*
wallet	cartera	*kar-TEH-ra*
(to) want	querer	*keh-REHR*
(I) want	(yo) quiero	*K'YEH-ro*
(you sg.) want	(Ud.) quiere	*K'YEH-reh*
(he, she) wants	(él, ella) quiere	*K'YEH-reh*
(we) want	(nosotros) queremos	*keh-REH-mohs*
(they, you pl.) want	quieren (ellos, ellas, Uds.)	*K'YEH-ren*
Do you (sg.) want . . . ?	¿Quiere Ud. . . . ? quieren	*¿K'YEH-reh oo-STED . . . ?*
war	guerra	*GHEH-rra*
warm	caliente	*ka-L'YEN-teh*
was (permanent status)	era	*EH-ra*
was (location or temporary status)	estaba	*ess-TA-ba*
(to) wash	lavar	*la-VAR*
watch	reloj (m)	*reh-LO*

Watch out!	¡Cuidado!	*¡kwee-DA-doh!*
water	el agua (f)	*AH-gwa*
water-color	acuarela	*ah-kwa-REH-la*
way (manner)	modo	*MO-doh*
way (road)	camino	*ka-MEE-no*
we	nosotros (m), nosotras (f)	*no-SO-trohs, no-SO-trahs*
weak	débil	*DEH-beel*
(to) wear	llevar	*l'yeh-VAR*
weather	tiempo	*T'YEM-po*
wedding	boda	*BO-da*
Wednesday	miércoles	*M'YER-ko-lehs*
week	semana	*seh-MA-na*
weekend	fin de semana (m)	*feen deh seh-MA-na*
(to) weigh	pesar	*peh-SAR*
weight	peso	*PEH-so*
Welcome!	¡Bienvenido!	*¡b'yen-veh-NEE-do!*
You are welcome	De nada	*deh NA-da*
well (adv.)	bien	*b'yen.*
well (water, oil)	pozo	*PO-so*
went		
(I) went	(yo) fui	*fwee*
(he, she, you sg.) went	(él, ella, Ud.) fue	*fweh*

(we) went	(nosotros) fuimos	FWEE-mohs
(they, you pl.) went	(ellos, ellas, Uds.) fueron	FWEH-rohn

were (permanent status)

(you sg.) were	(Ud.) era	EH-ra
(we) were	(nosotros) éramos	EH-ra-mohs
(they, you pl.) were	(ellos, ellas, Uds.) eran	EH-rahn

were (location or temporary status)

(you sg.) were	(Ud.) estaba	ess-TA-ba
(we) were	(nosotros) estábamos	ess-TA-ba-mohs
(they, you pl.) were	(ellos, ellas Uds.) estaban	ess-TA-bahn

west	oeste	oh-ESS-teh
what	que	keh
What's the matter?	¿Qué pasa?	¿keh PA-sa?
What time is it?	¿Qué hora es?	¿keh OH-ra ess?
What do you want?	¿Qué quiere Ud.?	¿keh K'YEH-reh oo-STED?
wheel	rueda	RWEH-da
when	cuando	KWAHN-doh
where	donde	DOHN-deh

wherever	dondequiera	*dohn-deh-K'YEH-ra*
Where to?	¿A dónde?	*ah DOHN-deh?*
whether	si	*see*
which	cual	*kwahl*
while	mientras	*M'YEN-trahs*
white	blanco	*BLAHN-ko*
who	quien	*k'yen*
whole	entero	*en-TEH-ro*
Whom?	¿A quién?	*¿ah k'yen?*
Why?	¿Por qué?	*¿por keh?*
Why not?	¿Por qué no?	*¿por keh no?*
wide	ancho	*AHN-cho*
widow	viuda	*V'YOO-da*
widower	viudo	*V'YOO-doh*
wife	esposa	*ess-PO-sa*
wild	salvaje	*sahl-VA-heh*

will

The future is formed by adding one of the following endings to the infinitive of the verb, according to the subject: (yo) -e (tú) -ás, (él, ella, Ud.) -á, (nosotros) -emos, (ellos, ellas, Uds.) -án.

I will speak	hablaré	*ah-bla-REH*
they won't speak	no hablarán	*no ah-bla-RAHN*
(to) win	ganar	*ga-NAR*
wind	viento	*V'YEN-toh*
window	ventana	*ven-TA-na*

wine	vino	*VEE-no*
winter	invierno	*een-V'YEHR-no*
(to) wish	desear	*deh-seh-AR*
without	sin	*seen*
wolf	lobo	*LO-bo*
woman	mujer	*moo-HEHR*
wonderful	maravilloso	*ma-ra-veel-YO-so*
won't (See "will.")		
wood	madera	*ma-DEH-ra*
woods	bosque (m)	*BOHS-keh*
wool	lana	*LA-na*
word	palabra	*pa-LA-bra*
work	trabajo	*tra-BA-ho*
(to) work	trabajar	*tra-ba-HAR*
world	mundo	*MOON-doh*
(to) worry	preocuparse	*pre-oh-koo-PAR-seh*
Don't worry.	No se preocupe.	*no seh pre-oh-KOO-peh.*
worse	peor	*peh-OR*

would:
Express the idea of "would" by adding the appropriate ending to the infinitive of the verb, according to the subject: (yo) -ía, (tú) -ías, (el, ella, Ud.) ía, (nosotros) -íamos, (ellos, ellas, Uds.) -ían.

I would speak	(yo) hablaría	*ah-bla-REE-ya*
I would learn	(yo) aprendería	*ah-pren-deh-REE-ya*

I would like . . .	Me gustaría . . .	*meh goos-ta-REE-ya . . .*
Would you like . . . ?	¿Le gustaría . . . ?	*¿leh goos-ta-REE-ya . . . ?*
wrist	muñeca	*moon-YEH-ka*
(to) write	escribir	*ess-kree-BEER*
Write it.	Escríbalo.	*ess-KREE-ba-lo.*
writer	escritor	*ess-kree-TOR*
wrong	equivocado	*eh-kee-vo-KA-doh*

Y

year	año	*AHN-yo*
yellow	amarillo	*ah-ma-REEL-yo*
yes	sí	*see*
yesterday	ayer	*ah-YEHR*
yet	todavía	*to-da-VEE-ya*
you	usted (sg.), ustedes (pl.) tú (fam.)	*oo-STED oo-STED-ehs*
young	joven	*HO-ven*
your	su	*soo*
yours	el suyo, la suya	*el SOO-yo, la SOO-ya*
yourself, yourselves (reflex.)	se	*seh*

Z

zipper	cierre (m)	*S'YEH-rreh*
zone	zona	*SO-na*
zoo	zoológico	*so-oh-LO-hee-ko*

Point to the Answer

For speedy reference and when in doubt, to get a clear answer to a question you have just asked, show the following Spanish pages to the person you are addressing and let *him* or *her* point to the answer to your question among the possible answers on these two pages.

A la persona con quien estoy hablando: Para esta seguro de haber sido comprendido le ruego señale la repuesta a mi pregunta. Muchas gracias.

To the person to whom I am speaking: To be sure to be understood I ask you to show here the answer to my question. Thank you very much.

| Sí. | No. | Quizás. |
| Yes. | No. | Perhaps. |

| Ciertamente. | Está bien. | Perdón. |
| Certainly. | All right. | Excuse me. |

| Comprendo. | | No comprendo. |
| I understand. | | I don't understand. |

| ¿Qué desea? | Yo sé. | No sé. |
| What do you want? | I know. | I don't know. |

| Otra vez. | | Es bastante. |
| Again (or more). | | Enough. |

Abierto.
Open.

Cerrado.
Closed.

Demasiado.
Too much.

No es suficiente.
Not enough.

Prohibido entrar.
No admittance.

Prohibido.
It is forbidden.

Propiedad privada.
Private property.

Ud. debe irse.
You must leave.

Ahora.
Now.

Más tarde.
Later.

Demasiado temprano.
Too early.

Demasiado.
tarde.
Too late.

Hoy.
Today.

Mañana.
Tomorrow.

Ayer.
Yesterday.

Esta noche.
Tonight.

Anoche.
Last night.

Mañana por la noche.
Tomorrow night.

Esta semana.
This week.

La semana
pasada.
Last week.

La semana que.
viene.
Next week.

Es posible.
It's possible.

No es posible.
It's not possible.

De acuerdo.
It is agreed.

Muy bien.
Very good.

No está
bien.
It isn't
good.

Es cerca.
It's near.

Demasiado
lejos.
Too far.

Muy lejos.
Very far.

Aquí.
Here.

Allá.
There.

Doble a la izquierda.
Turn left.

Doble a la derecha.
Turn right.

Siga derecho.	**Venga conmigo.**	**Sígame.**
Go straight ahead.	Come with me.	Follow me.

Vamos.	**Hemos llegado.**	**Pare aquí.**
Let's go.	We have arrived.	Stop here.

Espéreme.   **No puedo.**
Wait for me.   I cannot.

Esperaré.	**Debo irme.**	**Regrese más tarde.**
I will wait.	I must go.	Come back later.

Regreso en seguida.
I'll be right back.

Él no está aquí.	**Ella no está aquí.**
He is not here.	She is not here.

Mi nombre es ———.	**¿Su nombre?**
My name is ———.	Your name?

¿Número de teléfono?	**¿Dirección?**
Telephone number?	Address?

lunes	**martes**	**miércoles**	**jueves**
Monday	Tuesday	Wednesday	Thursday

viernes	**sábado**	**domingo**
Friday	Saturday	Sunday

A las ———.
At ——— o'clock.

Cuesta ——— pesos ——— centavos.
It costs ——— pesos ——— centavos.

uno	**dos**	**tres**	**cuatro**	**cinco**
one	two	three	four	five

seis	siete	ocho	nueve	diez
six	seven	eight	nine	ten

once	doce	trece	catorce	quince
eleven	twelve	thirteen	fourteen	fifteen

dieciséis	diecisiete	dieciocho
sixteen	seventeen	eighteen

diecinueve	veinte	treinta
nineteen	twenty	thirty

cuarenta	cincuenta	sesenta
forty	fifty	sixty

setenta	ochenta	noventa
seventy	eighty	ninety

cien	mil	diez mil
one hundred	one thousand	ten thousand